The Williamsburg
COOKBOOK

The Williamsburg
COOKBOOK

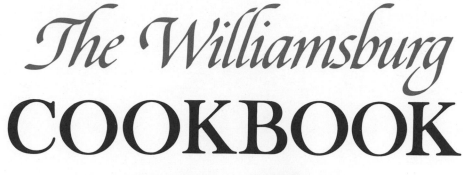

Traditional and Contemporary Recipes
Initially Compiled and Adapted by Letha Booth
Updated and Enlarged by the Staff
of Colonial Williamsburg

With Commentary by Joan Parry Dutton

Original Color Photography by Taylor Biggs Lewis, Jr.

Additional Color Photography by Bill Boxer

Line Drawings by Vernon Wooten

The Colonial Williamsburg Foundation

Williamsburg, Virginia

Updated and enlarged edition, 1975
Fourteenth printing, 2001
Printed in China

This book was designed by Vernon Wooten.

Library of Congress Cataloging in Publication Data

Booth, Letha, comp.
  The Williamsburg cookbook.

  Includes index.
  1. Cookery, American—Virginia. I. Colonial Williams-
burg Foundation. II. Title
TX715.725 1975   641.5'9755   75-2328
ISBN 0-910412-91-X hardbound
ISBN 0-910412-92-8 softbound

Cover:

*A pot of hearty Brunswick Stew is ready
for serving at Chowning's Tavern, complete
with all the fresh vegetables and tender
chicken that have made it a favorite with
Virginians for centuries.*

Frontispiece:

*In a colonial kitchen, chickens are golden-
brown on the spit, and a baked Virginia Ham
garnished with spiced fruits and watercress
is ready for the dinner table. The cook puts
a finishing touch on a cut of beef. In front
of the vegetables, left to right, are a Sally
Lunn, Apple Pie, and Indian Corn Sticks and
Muffins.*

Contents

Part I

Building a Tradition

Building a Tradition

For well over three centuries Virginia has been famed for its good food and hospitality. By 1699, when Williamsburg was founded, Virginians were enjoying a bill of fare that was probably unrivaled. The Tidewater, with its forests and its waterways, was a primeval paradise of fish and game, just as England, an island surrounded by fish, was once a vast game preserve. Domestic animals, brought over from England, thrived in the new climate, and so did English vegetables and fruits. Then there were the Indians' crops, above all their corn. The first settlers had brought wheat with them, but soon they were growing more corn than wheat.

Engaged one way or another in tobacco growing, almost all Virginians lived on the land. Williamsburg was small but beautiful, as befitted the seat of government. With no more than two thousand permanent residents, for most of the year it enjoyed quiet and ease. But during Publick Times, when the courts convened in the spring and fall, when the Assembly met, on royal birthdays, and on other special occasions, the town grew almost overnight. Williamsburg became the setting for carnival and for affairs of law and state. It was vibrant with color, dust,

1

and noise, agog with all the robustness and all the elegance of Virginia's Golden Age.

To cope with such regular invasions, an extraordinary number of "convenient ordinaries or inns for accommodation of strangers" offered meals, drinks, and lodging. The taverns of Williamsburg, like the taverns of London in those days, played an integral part in town life. Their patrons were councillors and burgesses, ship captains and lawyers, merchants and planters, who met within their doors to transact business, talk politics, play cards, and gossip over a bottle of wine, a bowl of punch, or a tankard of ale.

The tavern-keeper was a man of consequence. He received his guests in the true manner of a host, discussed with them matters of moment, and judged when to keep his counsel and when to disclose it. Above all, each tavern-keeper was expected to provide his patrons with a bill of fare (a choice of fish, meat, fruits, and vegetables in season) and a choice of wines comparable to those served by planters at home. Only those taverns with good cooks in the kitchen survived.

Virginians, being mostly of English and Scottish stock, ate much the same kind of food as did Britons. English cookbooks were the Virginia housewife's standby. Two of the most popular eighteenth-century cookbooks used in Virginia were *The Art of Cookery Made Plain and Easy* by Mrs. Hannah Glasse and *The Compleat Housewife* by Mrs. E. Smith. First published in London in 1727, *The Compleat Housewife* was reprinted by William Parks of Williamsburg in 1742. It was the first cookbook published in British America.

A copy of William Parks's reprint belonging to the Virginia Historical Society was rebound by C. Clement Samford, Williamsburg's master bookbinder, 222 years after the book was first sold. Samford gave it a new brown calfskin cover and matching end sheets of old paper; the interior pages were in exceptionally good condition.

Bookbinding is but one of the traditional crafts still being carried on in Williamsburg. Others are to be seen in the many craft shops and outdoor demonstrations. The exhibition buildings and taverns in the Historic Area, like the town itself, are even busier now than they were in colonial days, for not only Virginians but presidents of the United States, foreign heads of state, and visitors from all walks of life and most parts of the world come to what was the capital of colonial Virginia.

Four eighteenth-century taverns, the King's Arms, Christiana Campbell's, Josiah Chowning's, and Shields, provide dining facilities for visitors. (Colonial Williamsburg's entirely modern Williamsburg Inn,

Williamsburg Lodge, Woodlands hotel and restaurant, and Governor's Inn, just outside the limits of the Historic Area, provide both meals and lodging beyond any early traveler's imagination.) In each of the taverns, the chairs, tables, and tableware reflect colonial styles in furnishings. The people who welcome and wait on visitors in the candlelit dining rooms wear colonial dress. The amenities that restaurateurs require—the modern cookstoves, refrigerators, and cooking utensils—are all behind the scenes.

Menus, printed in old-style Caslon, a typeface much used in America in colonial times, list modern dishes along with the old familiar southern foods: chowders, fried chicken, spoon bread and cornsticks, pecan pie, and the Tidewater's specialties—Virginia ham and Sally Lunn.

Many of the recipes in this book are derived from those that our great-great-grandmothers used; others are in the tradition of southern cooking; and some blend the tastes of the Old World and the New. Mrs. Letha Booth was an important part of the Williamsburg tradition. She was the manager of Travis House, Colonial Williamsburg's first restaurant in the eighteenth-century manner, from 1946 until 1951, and thereafter until her retirement she managed the famous King's Arms Tavern. Most of the recipes in this book were initially compiled and adapted for the home kitchen by Mrs. Booth. Others have been added and similarly adapted by more recent members of the Colonial

3

Williamsburg restaurant operations staff. All were written and retested by Mrs. Grace Sumner, Norfolk food editor. The Shields Tavern Sampler recipes, which come from popular eighteenth-century British and Virginia cookbooks, were tested in Colonial Williamsburg's exhibition kitchens using eighteenth-century equipment and methods and were adapted for twentieth-century use by Ms. Rosemary Brandau, manager, Historic Food Programs.

Selected Menus for Various
and Special Occasions

Meals Fit for a King—
or a Queen

Many foreign heads of state invited by the president of the United States for an official visit to this country come to Williamsburg. The visit gives them a chance to see something of what colonial America was like and to spend a quiet evening following the long flights from their homelands before being whisked off by helicopter the next morning to be set down on the White House lawn.

On the last lap of a three-week tour of the eastern United States in 1957, Queen Elizabeth and Prince Philip came to Williamsburg, at the invitation of Governor Thomas B. Stanley of Virginia, to attend the 350th anniversary celebration of the founding of Jamestown. Colonial Williamsburg's dinner in their honor was most carefully planned. By discreet inquiries their hosts in Williamsburg learned the royal couple's eating preferences, as noted along their route, and the menu that was to be presented to them in Washington the day before, as well as that in New York City the following day.

The dinner set before them, compared with the lavishness of colonial entertaining, was simple, but it did include some traditional dishes in modern dress. In her letter of thanks Queen Elizabeth wrote that she and Prince Philip had enjoyed that dinner more than any other dinner in their travels anywhere.

Dinner in honor of Her Majesty, Queen Elizabeth II and His Royal Highness, Prince Philip Williamsburg Inn

Clear Green Turtle Soup, Amontillado*   *Cheese Straws*

Mushrooms Bordelaise
(Williams and Humbert Dry Sack)

Boneless Breast of Chicken with Virginia Ham*
Baby Green Beans, Amandine
(Bâtard Montrachet, 1953)

Avocado Slices   *French Dressing**

Fresh Strawberry Mousse*
(Veuve Clicquot Yellow Label, Dry)

Demitasse and Liqueurs

In colonial days it was customary for royal governors to celebrate British sovereigns' birthnights. On a May evening in 1976, the members of the British Bicentennial Heritage Mission were invited to a supper at the Governor's Palace to honor one of their number, the Earl of Dunmore, and to mark the first time a descendant of a royal governor of Virginia had dined at the Palace since Virginia became a commonwealth. The Earl's ancestor, the 4th Earl of Dunmore, was the last royal governor of Virginia. He fled the colony in 1775, ending 168 years of British rule.

The affair was much in the spirit of a party Governor and Lady Dunmore gave on the evening of January 18, 1775, the birthnight of Queen Charlotte.

WEDNESDAY last being the day for celebrating the birth of her Majesty, his Excellency the Earl of Dunmore gave a

* *Recipe is in this cookbook; see index for page number.*

ball and elegant entertainment at the Palace to a numerous company of Ladies and Gentlemen. The same day his Lordship's youngest daughter was baptised in the name VIRGINIA.

The supper was similar to those served in the governor's house in the eighteenth century. Governor Dunmore had large farm holdings that provided a wide variety of meats, fruits, and vegetables. The entertainment was colonial in style also. Musicians, singers, a conjurer, a juggler, and several acrobats added to the gaiety of the evening.

Supper given for the British Bicentennial Heritage Mission in honor of the Earl of Dunmore Governor's Palace

Cold Plantation Beef
(Château St. Paul, Haut-Médoc)

Roast Virginia Quail, Peach Garnish*
King's Arms Tavern Sweet Potatoes*

Garden Salad Greens
Stilton Cheese

Bicentennial Tart*
(Charles Heidsieck, Brut)

Demitasse and Cordials

* Recipe is in this cookbook; see index for page number.

Meals Fit for a King—or a Queen

**Dinner in honor of Their Majesties
The King and Queen of Thailand
King's Arms Tavern**

A Dish of Chesapeake Bay *Crabmeat, artfully
arranged in natural Shell**

Boneless Breast of Rockingham County *Chicken, fried brown,
with Curls of* Surry County *Ham*

A Variety of choice Vegetables from the Tavern Garden

Greengage Plums jellied in Chablis *Wine
from an eighteenth-century Receipt
brought out from* London

Sally Lunn*   Indian *Corn Muffins**

*A Fig Ice Cream**
*devised from an eighteenth-century Receipt
brought out from* Paris

King's Arms Confections

Demitasse

Bâtard Montrachet, 1955   *Bollinger, Brut*

* *Recipe is in this cookbook; see index for page number.*

Family Meals, Then and Now

By our standards, family meals in the old days were prodigious. Not necessarily for the quantity of food consumed, for many of the colony's leading men ate sparingly, but for the variety of dishes on hand.

Tidewater Virginians continued the English custom of a hearty breakfast, usually between eight and nine o'clock, of venison, game or poultry, and ham. A new item was the fresh-baked hot breads, often Indian cakes, in what came to be recognized as "the Virginia fashion." Dinner was from around half-past two to four. The choice of dishes was wide: beef, roast pig, mutton, fish, ham of course, greens, and a pudding and cheese to round it off. Supper was light, took place about eight, and usually consisted of oysters, "battered" eggs, or bread and cheese, wine or cider, fruit, and some light dessert.

The dining table was indeed a groaning board, for families were larger in those days and Virginians kept open house to an extraordinary

Champagne toasts welcome the new year at the Williamsburg Inn. Featured foods include, counterclockwise, Marinated Shrimp in Fresh Dill; Barbecued Baby Spareribs; Biscuits Spread with Virginia Ham Pâté; Cheddar Cheese and Olive Balls; Peanuts; Skewered Pineapple and Strawberries in Kirsch; and Chilled Backfin Crabmeat. ▶

degree. Kith and kin arriving unexpectedly might stay for weeks at a time, and even a passing stranger was welcome.

Our way of living, and consequently our eating habits, are now vastly different. Today's family menus reflect the change.

*Chowning's Tavern Brunswick Stew**

Salad of Mixed Greens   *Manchet Bread**
*with Oil and Vinegar Dressing**

*Wine Jelly Mold with Custard Sauce**

⋅≼⊱⊰≽⋅

Virginia Ham and Brandied Peaches**

*Carrot Pudding**   *Green Beans*

*King's Arms Tavern Greengage Plum Ice Cream**

*Cinnamon Squares**

⋅≼⊱⊰≽⋅

*Ginger Beef**

Steamed Rice   *Brussels Sprouts*

*Lemon Chess Tarts**

⋅≼⊱⊰≽⋅

*Chesapeake Oyster Bisque**

*Williamsburg Inn Breast of Turkey Supreme**

Rice or Noodles   *Scalloped Tomatoes and Artichoke Hearts**

*Apple Pie**

* *Recipe is in this cookbook; see index for page number.*

◄   *At Shields Tavern, a sampler of 1740s foods*
tempts patrons with such tasty victuals as
(clockwise) Shields Onion Soup, Fricassee of
Chicken, Indian Meal Pudding, Carrot Puff,
and Meat Patty in Crust.

Building a Tradition

*Baked Eggs in Casserole**
*Mixed Fruit Salad with Williamsburg Inn Honey Dressing**
*Williamsburg Lodge Orange Wine Cake**

❦

*King's Arms Tavern Cream of Peanut Soup**
*Christiana Campbell's Tavern Salmagundi**
*Sally Lunn**
*Raspberry Ice**   *Williamsburg Inn Pecan Bars**

❦

*Shields Tavern Chicken with Virginia Apple Dressing**
Green Peas with Whole Onions
*Fresh Garden Stuff with French Dressing**
*Shields Tavern Syllabub**

❦

*Chowning's Tavern Sautéed Backfin Crabmeat**
*Christiana Campbell's Tavern Spoon Bread**
Buttered Fresh Asparagus
*Christiana Campbell's Tavern Tipsy Squire**

* Recipe is in this cookbook; see index for page number.

12

Family Meals, Then and Now

Shields Tavern Onion Soup*
Cascades Baked Stuffed Flounder*
Cascades Ratatouille*
*Salad of Boston Lettuce with Williamsburg Inn
Regency Dressing**
Christiana Campbell's Tavern Rum Cream Pie*

Melon Balls with Virginia Ham*
Travis House Oysters*
Indian Corn Sticks*
Salad of Mixed Greens with Garlic French Dressing*
Black Forest Cake*

* Recipe is in this cookbook; see index for page number.

Christmas Feast and Festival

In Williamsburg not only Christmas itself but the Christmas season—
as it was called in colonial days—is observed. In the twentieth century, this festive holiday period extends from mid-December until early
in January.

True, the festivities of today are more elaborate than they were in
colonial days. Then Christmas was primarily a religious festival. However, toward the end of the colonial period balls, foxhunts, and the
firing of the Christmas guns were part and parcel of the holiday season,
and there is evidence that plantation owners' wives concerned themselves and lent a hand in the making of what had become traditional
holiday fare. Nor were friends in England forgotten. In August 1770,
with forethought of the time it took a sailing ship to make the Atlantic
crossing, Mrs. Martha Goosley and Mrs. Mary Ambler of Yorktown
sent to John Norton, merchant of London, two Christmas turkeys and
"hams to eat with them."

Today, Colonial Williamsburg keeps what most of us think of as the
old-style Christmas. Old English customs, the yule-log ceremony and

the wassail bowl, have been revived. Adapted from the German custom, a living evergreen serves proudly as a Christmas tree on Market Square. With a candle in every window and a wreath on every door, the Historic Area is aglow, and there is music in the air. Rich seasonal fare, a blend of traditional and relatively newly devised dishes, is offered by the taverns and restaurants.

The Groaning Board, which combines delicious food with delightful entertainment, is a feast for all five senses. True, roast prime rib of beef and southern fried chicken have been substituted for the boar's head that was the traditional Christmas dish in medieval England. Armed with tusks and elaborately decorated, the boar's head was paraded ceremoniously around the great hall in the castle before being partaken of by the baron's favored guests. Twentieth-century tastes now favor such treats as cream of oyster and spinach soup, poached fillet of flounder with creole sauce, and cherry trifle.

The enjoyment of feasting at the Groaning Board is enhanced by minstrels and madrigal singers who play and sing tunes that were popular in eighteenth-century Virginia. Costumed colonial dancers also perform, and everyone present joins in the revelry that celebrates the Christmas season in Williamsburg.

Christmas Day

Wassail*   *Cheese Wafers**

Williamsburg Inn Chilled Crab Gumbo*

Roast Young Tom Turkey

Fresh Mushroom Dressing

King's Arms Tavern   *Hearts of Lettuce*
Creamed Celery with Pecans*   *Roquefort French Dressing**

Eggnog Pie*

and/or

Ambrosia*   *Mince Pie with Rum Butter Sauce**

* *Recipe is in this cookbook; see index for page number.*

Building a Tradition

The Groaning Board

Cream of Oyster and Spinach Soup*
King's Arms Tavern Poached Fillet of Flounder with Creole Sauce*
Steamed Rice
Roast Prime Rib of Beef
Southern Fried Chicken
Corn Pudding*
Zucchini with Onions and Tomatoes
Salmagundi*
Chowning's Tavern Loaf
Sally Lunn*
Cherry Trifle*

❧❦❧

A New Year's Eve Cocktail Party

Chilled Backfin Crabmeat with Mayonnaise*
Cheddar Cheese and Olive Balls*
Barbecued Baby Spareribs*
Marinated Shrimp in Fresh Dill*
Skewered Pineapple and Strawberries in Kirsch*
Biscuits Spread with Virginia Ham Pâté*

* Recipe is in this cookbook; see index for page number.

Tavern Fare

Christiana Campbell's Tavern

Mrs. Christiana Campbell kept the tavern that bears her name from 1771 to 1776. From a contemporary description it seems that Mrs. Campbell was certainly no beauty, but she was an excellent manager and had a way of knowing and remembering just what each patron especially liked. George Washington, then a burgess, recorded that he had dined at Mrs. Campbell's twenty-seven times during one session of the General Assembly, and supped and spent many an evening besides under her roof. Among Colonial Williamsburg's prized possessions is a receipt for payment for food and drink given by George Washington to Christiana Campbell on April 8, 1772.

Situated behind the Capitol, Christiana Campbell's Tavern today features seafood from the Chesapeake Bay.

17

Bill of Fare at Christiana Campbell's Tavern

BRUNCH FARE
Christiana Campbell's TAVERN
Giving Satisfaction to TRAVELERS and TOWNSPEOPLE with a Taste for SEAFOODS

APPETIZERS

FRUIT *Ambrosia*   Mulled Apple CIDER   Captain *Rasmussen's* CLAM Chowder   Orange JUICE or Tomato JUICE

French ONION SOUP with *Swiss* CHEESE and Toasted CROUTON

Mrs. *Campbell's* Favorite BREAKFAST
Mulled Apple CIDER
A Taste of *Virginia* HAM,
Southern Fried CHICKEN, and Scrambled EGGS
Choice of BEVERAGE

Fisherman's BREAKFAST
Captain *Rasmussen's* CLAM Chowder
Two CRAB Cakes
Served with *Campbell's* Cabbage SLAW
and Tartar Sauce

Southern Fried CHICKEN
Served with *Campbell's*
Cabbage SLAW
and a Spiced PEACH

CHICKEN and LEEK Pie
Boneless Breast of CHICKEN Combined
with Fresh LEEKS and a mild Supreme SAUCE
Topped with a PASTRY Shell

Pecan WAFFLES
and Country SAUSAGE
Served with Warm Maple
SYRUP

Grilled CHICKEN Hash
Served on Manchet Toast
Topped with
a Poached EGG
and Spiced
TOMATO Sauce

SALMAGUNDI
An Eighteenth-Century Chef's SALAD Combining
Fresh Garden GREENS, *VIRGINIA* HAM,
TURKEY, *Cheddar* CHEESE, Hard-Cooked EGGS,
CELERY Hearts, ANCHOVIES, OLIVES, and
Mrs. *Campbell's* Salad DRESSING

Hot Corned BEEF and
Swiss CHEESE Sandwich
Served on a Fresh RYE Roll
with *Dijon* MUSTARD—
HORSERADISH Sauce, and
CABBAGE Slaw

Meals Served with Hot Drop Biscuits and Sweet Potato MUFFINS

CHEF'S BRUNCH SPECIAL
Priced Daily

❀ Our Special OMELETS ❀

Backfin CRAB and Cheddar CHEESE with White Wine SAUCE
VIRGINIA HAM and *Cheddar* CHEESE
The Combination OMELET — A Mixture of ONION, Green PEPPERS,
and Fresh MUSHROOMS Topped with a Rich *Jambalaya* SAUCE

All Served with Fried POTATO Wedges and a Broiled TOMATO

BEVERAGES
COFFEE, MILK, TEA (Hot or Iced), LEMONADE

DESSERTS

Poached PEAR in Port WINE
Mrs. *Campbell's* BREAD PUDDING
Rum Cream PIE with CHOCOLATE
Shavings
Lemon or Raspberry SHERBET

Warm Apple TURNOVER with Nutmeg SAUCE
Seasonal Selection of PIES — Ask your WAITER
Campbell's Fig ICE CREAM
Vanilla or Chocolate ICE CREAM

Children's MENU Available —
Ask your WAITER

Recipes for many of these foods are included in either The *Williamsburg Cookbook* or *Favorite Meals From Williamsburg: A Menu Cookbook.* Both books are available here at the tavern. Please ask your waiter.

King's Arms Tavern

Mrs. Jane Vobe kept tavern at various locations in Williamsburg for thirty-three years, longer, so far as is known, than anyone else. First recorded as keeping tavern in 1752, she opened a new tavern "at the sign of the King's Arms" on Duke of Gloucester Street in 1772, and presumably retired in 1785, when she advertised the King's Arms for rent. She sold tickets for theater performances, invited artists to display their pictures in the tavern, posted rewards for the return of articles lost by guests, and prided herself on attracting a clientele as select as any in town.

The present-day King's Arms continues to serve the best. Here Colonial Williamsburg has entertained among others the king and queen of Thailand, the lord mayor of London and his lady, the president of the Argentine Republic, England's Queen Mother Elizabeth, and King Baudouin of the Belgians.

Chowning's Tavern

Josiah Chowning opened his tavern in 1766 for humbler folk or ordinary people, as he put it, assuring them they could "depend upon the best of entertainment for themselves, servants and horses, and good pasturage." He prided himself on his good bread. On Chowning's bill of fare the word "sippets" describes strips of dry toast. The sandwiches are made from hand-sliced bread, which is why a neighbor's sandwich may be slightly thicker or thinner than your own.

Chowning's Tavern retains much of its original character, that of an alehouse of old. Of the three taverns, its atmosphere is nearest to that of an English village pub. Draft ale, beer, and other spiritous beverages are served. Students from the College of William and Mary like to go there for "Chowning's good Bread" (a loaf-sized round) with butter and a glass of cider—served ice cold in summer under the grapevine covered arbor, or mulled and spiced in winter before the fireplace.

Chowning's Tavern Evening Fare

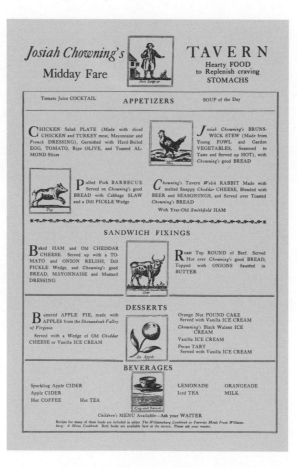

Shields TAVERN

E V E N I N G   M E N U

A P P E T I Z E R S

Shields Cream of Crayfish SOUP

SOUP of the DAY

Shields SAMPLER – A Tasting of the 1700s FOODS

Cherrystone CLAMS on the Half Shell

Rappahannock OYSTERS on the Half Shell

Buttered CRABMEAT with SIPPETS and RELISHES

E N T R É E S

One-half Barnyard CHICKEN Roasted on a Spit,
served with Red Bliss POTATOES

Baked Red SNAPPER with Shrimp SAUCE,
served with Red Bliss POTATOES and
VEGETABLE of the DAY

Poached *Chesapeake Bay* SEAFOOD PLATTER
with Butter Sauce, Pecan HUSH PUPPIES, and
VEGETABLE

Broiled PEPPERCORN STEAK with Sautéed
ONIONS and Fresh MUSHROOMS

Baked PORK CHOP with *Virginia* Apple
FRITTERS

Roasted Prime RIB of BEEF with Garden
VEGETABLES and Baked POTATO

Each Entrée Served with Special *Shields* ROLL and
Tossed Fresh Garden GREENS with *Shields* DRESSING
OR a DISH of Seasonal Fresh FRUITS

Shields Tavern

In the early 1740s James Shields took over the tavern that his Huguenot father-in-law, John Marot, had operated several decades earlier. Shields likely made extensive renovations and added the small wing to the east in order to attract well-to-do customers who frequented Wetherburn's and the Raleigh taverns. Although located close to the Capitol, Shields Tavern attracted lower gentry and middling customers.

Shields Tavern became Colonial Williamsburg's fourth operating tavern in early 1989. Present-day visitors dine in a setting that depicts tavern keeping during the first half of the eighteenth century. The menu features crayfish soup, spit-roasted meats, a sampler of 1740s foods, and syllabub and other traditional desserts.

Part II

Recipes

Appetizers

The appetizer, which came in with Prohibition to accompany what was often an unpalatable drink and stayed on in favor as companion to the cocktail, nowadays takes first place on the menu, and is a new course.

BARBECUED BABY SPARERIBS

(4–6 servings)

5 pounds baby spareribs   curry powder
salt and pepper to taste   BARBECUE SAUCE *(page 93)*

Preheat the oven to 400° F.

Prepare the spareribs by removing excess fat and cutting them into as many pieces as desired.

Place the spareribs, flesh side up, on a rack in a shallow roasting pan.

Sprinkle with salt, pepper, and very lightly with curry powder.

Bake the spareribs at 400° F. for 1 hour, basting with warm Barbecue Sauce every 10 minutes.

When the spareribs are done, brush with the remaining Barbecue Sauce and serve.

CHEDDAR CHEESE AND OLIVE BALLS

(36–40 balls)

¼ pound Cheddar cheese   ¾ cup all-purpose flour
¼ cup butter, softened   36 to 40 small stuffed green
¼ teaspoon paprika   olives, drained

Preheat the oven to 375° F. 10 minutes before the cheese balls are to go in.

Grate the cheese and allow it to soften to room temperature.

Combine the cheese, butter, and paprika.

Mix well into the flour, by hand, until the pieces of cheese disappear and the mixture is smooth and deep yellow in color.

Cover and allow it to stand at room temperature 15 minutes.

Pinch off small pieces of dough (about 1 teaspoon) and flatten in palm of hand to a circle about 1½ inches in diameter.

Place a well-drained olive in the center of the dough, bringing the edges together to cover the olive completely. Roll gently between palms of hands.

Place on an ungreased cookie sheet; chill 10 minutes in the refrigerator.

Bake at 375° F. for 20 to 25 minutes or until lightly browned. Serve hot.

Note: May be made in advance and frozen before baking. Bake frozen, about 30 minutes. Do not thaw.

CHEESE WAFERS
(3 dozen)

1 cup all-purpose flour
1 teaspoon salt
½ teaspoon ginger
⅓ cup shortening
1 cup grated sharp cheese,
    packed

¼ cup toasted sesame seeds
½ teaspoon Worcestershire
    sauce
2 to 3 tablespoons ice water

Preheat the oven to 400° F. 10 minutes before the wafers are to go in.

Grease cookie sheets.

Combine all ingredients and work into a smooth dough.

Divide the dough in half, making 2 rolls about 8 inches long and 1¼ inches in diameter, and put them in the refrigerator to chill.

When firm, slice into wafers ⅛ inch thick.

Place on prepared cookie sheets and prick with a fork.

Bake at 400° F. for 10 to 12 minutes.

SHIELDS TAVERN SAMPLER
MEAT PATTIES IN CRUST
(3 dozen)

3 to 4 sheets frozen puff
    pastry
1 cup VIRGINIA HAM *(page*
    47) or smoked ham, cooked
    and ground
½ pound veal or beef, cooked,
    ground, and drained
    (approximately 1 cup)

1 tablespoon fresh parsley,
    chopped
½ teaspoon thyme leaves
1 teaspoon nutmeg, freshly
    ground
½ teaspoon pepper

Follow the directions on the package to thaw the frozen puff pastry.

Preheat the oven to 350° F.

Combine the ham with the veal or beef. Season the meat mixture with the parsley, thyme, nutmeg, and pepper.

Cut the puff pastry into 3-inch squares.

Spoon approximately 1 tablespoon of the meat mixture onto each square. Fold the squares in half to form triangles and press the edges together firmly.

Place the patties on a cookie sheet. Bake at 350° F. for 15 to 20 minutes until golden brown.

CHILLED BACKFIN CRABMEAT WITH MAYONNAISE

(4–6 servings)

1 pound backfin crabmeat,
  chilled
2 tablespoons lemon juice
salt and pepper to taste

½ cup mayonnaise
1 head of lettuce (Boston or
  Bibb)

Pick over the chilled crabmeat and discard any bits of shell or cartilage.

Season with lemon juice, salt, and pepper.

Gently fold in the mayonnaise.

Serve in lettuce cups.

MARINATED SHRIMP
IN FRESH DILL
(8–10 servings)

1 quart water
1 tablespoon salt
1 teaspoon dill weed
1 lemon, sliced

2½ pounds shrimp in shell
MARINADE OF FRESH DILL
(below)

Bring salted water, dill weed, and sliced lemon to a boil.

Add the shrimp and simmer until the shrimp are pink, about 3 to 4 minutes.

Immediately drain and chill the shrimp.

Peel and devein the shrimp and place them in a crock or bowl.

Pour Marinade of Fresh Dill over the shrimp; cover and store in the refrigerator for 24 hours.

MARINADE OF FRESH DILL

½ cup olive oil
½ cup dry white wine
4 teaspoons fresh dill,
  chopped
1 teaspoon pepper, freshly
  ground

dash of garlic powder
2 drops Tabasco sauce
½ cup lemon juice
salt to taste
1 tablespoon chives, snipped

Mix all ingredients well. Pour over the shrimp.

MELON BALLS WITH VIRGINIA HAM

(24–36 balls)

6 to 8 ounces Virginia Ham
(page 47), very thinly sliced

*1 medium honeydew, large
 cantaloupe, or Spanish
 melon*
toothpicks

Slice the ham into thin strips about 1 inch wide x 4 inches long.

Cut the melon into balls approximately 1 inch in diameter with a melon ball cutter.

Place the melon balls on paper toweling to absorb the moisture.

Wrap each melon ball with a strip of ham and secure with a toothpick.

Chill and serve.

OYSTERS WITH BACON

(1 dozen)

6 slices bacon
*1 teaspoon Worcestershire
 sauce*

salt and pepper to taste
1 tablespoon lemon juice
12 fresh oysters
toothpicks

Preheat the oven to 400° F.

Cut the bacon strips in half and fry until partially done; drain.

Combine the seasonings. Season the oysters and wrap each oyster in half a slice of bacon; secure with a toothpick.

Bake at 400° F. on a rack over a shallow pan for 5 to 7 minutes or until the bacon is done. Serve hot.

SKEWERED PINEAPPLE
AND STRAWBERRIES IN KIRSCH

(8–10 servings)

1 fresh pineapple, well ripened
*1 quart (40 to 50) fresh
 strawberries*

½ cup kirsch
bamboo skewers as needed

Peel and cube the fresh pineapple.

Pick over the strawberries, wash, and hull.

Place the pineapple cubes and strawberries in a bowl; sprinkle with kirsch.

Chill at least 30 minutes, turning several times.

Serve the pineapple and strawberries on skewers.

VIRGINIA HAM BISCUITS

(40 regular or 70 cocktail)

milk
1 recipe MRS. BOOTH'S
  BISCUIT MIX *(page 113)*
melted butter

1¼ to 1½ pounds VIRGINIA
  HAM *(page 47), very thinly
  sliced*

Preheat the oven to 425° F.

Grease cookie sheets.

Using a fork, stir enough milk into the biscuit mix to make a soft but not sticky dough.

Knead on a lightly floured board until the dough is smooth and elastic.

Roll out ¼ inch thick, then fold dough over so that the biscuits will open easily when baked.

Cut with a 1½- or 2-inch biscuit cutter, place on prepared cookie sheets, and brush the tops with melted butter or milk.

Bake at 425° F. for 8 to 10 minutes or until golden brown.

Place pieces of ham in the biscuits and serve warm.

Note: Biscuits and ham can be put together ahead of time. Wrap in aluminum foil and reheat before serving.

BISCUITS SPREAD
WITH VIRGINIA HAM PÂTÉ
(40 regular or 70 cocktail)

milk
1 recipe MRS. BOOTH'S
   BISCUIT MIX *(page 113)*
melted butter
¼ cup French-style prepared
   mustard

½ cup mayonnaise
1 pound VIRGINIA HAM *(page
   47), finely ground*

Follow the instructions under Virginia Ham Biscuits (page 30) to make the biscuits.

Add the mustard and mayonnaise to very finely ground ham; mix thoroughly.

Spread on hot biscuits; serve warm.

Note: As an alternative serving suggestion, the ham mixture may be rolled into small balls (about 1 teaspoon) with a peanut in the center, rolled in fine bread crumbs, and fried quickly in deep hot fat until golden brown. Drain well and serve warm.

Soups and Stews

An "excellent Soupe" made of venison and turkey moved William Byrd II to an unusual metaphor: "It never cloy'd, no more than an Engaging Wife wou'd do, by being a Constant Dish."

Eighteenth-century men were not the only admirers of good soup. President Harry S. Truman, who visited Williamsburg during his years in the White House, liked the soup served him at the Inn so well that he sent a message of congratulations to the chef. "One day I'll slip back for more—only nobody will know I'm here."

Soups are, broadly speaking, either thick or clear. In colonial days thick soups were favored. Modern gastronomes would call for a consommé or clear soup for a festive dinner.

A Williamsburg guest in 1946, Sir Winston Churchill so liked the Clear Green Turtle Soup Amontillado served him at the dinner in his honor at the Inn that he asked for more. Resting afterward in his room before boarding an after-midnight special train to take him back to Washington, he asked if a tureen of the same turtle consommé could be sent up to his room. The kitchen was closed, but the chef was still around, and soon a full tureen was sent to the statesman's room.

A decade later, the same Clear Green Turtle Soup Amontillado Sir Winston Churchill so relished was served at the Inn to Queen Elizabeth and Prince Philip.

When asked for the secret of his good soups, Fred Crawford, chef at the Inn for many years, replied instantly, "It's the way the ingredients are put together and the seasonings." This was, perhaps, an oversimplified way of saying that nothing can be taken out of a pot which does not first go in. If the base of a soup is not just right, no amount of boiling and simmering can put it right. The art of cookery lies in the blending and proportions of the seasonings.

CLEAR GREEN TURTLE SOUP
AMONTILLADO
(*12–15 servings*)

Bouquet garni:
½ teaspoon basil
½ teaspoon marjoram
½ teaspoon rosemary
½ teaspoon thyme
½ teaspoon fennel seeds
½ teaspoon mint
½ teaspoon sage
½ teaspoon allspice

1 jar (2¼ ounces) beef-flavored instant bouillon beads
1 can (28 ounces) green turtle meat
salt and pepper to taste
amontillado sherry

Prepare a bouquet garni by tying the herbs in a cheesecloth bag.

Dissolve the bouillon beads in 1 gallon of water, bring to a boil, and reduce the heat to simmer.

Add the bouquet garni and simmer 15 minutes.

Drain the juice from the turtle meat and reserve; add the juice to the stock.

Simmer at least 30 minutes, skimming the froth from the stock occasionally.

Cut the turtle meat into small cubes.

Remove the stock from the heat and strain it through a double thickness of cheesecloth. Return to the heat and add the turtle meat and salt and pepper to taste.

Add the sherry to taste, about 1 tablespoon, to each individual portion before serving.

SHIELDS TAVERN SAMPLER
ONION SOUP

(*6–8 servings*)

5 medium onions, chopped
¼ pound butter
1 tablespoon all-purpose flour
4 cups boiling water

1 cup stale bread crumbs
1½ teaspoons salt
1 egg yolk
1½ teaspoons vinegar

Sauté the onions in the butter for about 15 minutes.

Shake the flour into the onions, stirring continuously. Shake the pan and cook a few minutes.

Stir in the boiling water.

Add the bread crumbs and salt. Cook 10 minutes, stirring continuously.

Remove the onion mixture from the heat.

Beat the egg yolk with the vinegar.

Stir about ⅓ cup of the hot onion mixture into the egg mixture. Then stir the egg mixture back into the soup. Mix well and serve.

Note: A pinch of thyme adds a nice flavor to the soup.

Shields Onion Soup is especially delicious if made a day ahead of time.

BEEF BROTH
WITH TOMATOES AND OKRA
(*6 servings*)

1 soup bone	*pinch of leaf oregano*
1 pound ground beef	*3 cups canned tomatoes*
1 pound stewing beef	*1 cup okra, cut*
3 ribs of celery with leaves, chopped	*2 tablespoons cornstarch*
2 medium onions, sliced	*salt and pepper to taste*
1 large bay leaf	*dash of Worcestershire sauce*

Put the soup bone, ground beef, stewing beef, celery, onions, bay leaf, and oregano into a kettle with 2 quarts of water and simmer, uncovered, for 1½ hours.

Remove the stewing beef and dice it.

Strain the stock. Skim off the fat.

Add the diced stewing beef, tomatoes, and okra to the strained stock and return to the heat.

Mix the cornstarch with a little cold water and add it to the stock, stirring until evenly blended.

Add the seasonings and simmer, uncovered, for 20 minutes.

Serve very hot.

KING'S ARMS TAVERN
CREAM OF PEANUT SOUP
(10–12 servings)

Brazil is the native home of the peanut, the "ground nut" that sailed with Portuguese explorers to Africa and back to the Americas with the Negro. In 1794, Thomas Jefferson recorded the yield of sixty-five peanut hills at Monticello. The cultivation of peanuts increased in the South in the nineteenth century, but it was not until after the Civil War that they gained national acceptance.

Peanut soup is comparatively new, but it is much in demand in the King's Arms Tavern.

1 medium onion, chopped	*(page 45), or canned*
2 ribs of celery, chopped	*chicken broth*
¼ cup butter	*2 cups smooth peanut butter*
3 tablespoons all-purpose	*1¾ cups light cream*
flour	*peanuts, chopped*
2 quarts CHICKEN STOCK	

Sauté the onion and the celery in butter until soft, but not brown.

Stir in the flour until well blended.

Add the Chicken Stock, stirring constantly, and bring to a boil.

Remove from the heat and purée in a food processor or a blender.

Add the peanut butter and cream, stirring to blend thoroughly.

Return to low heat and heat until just hot, but do not boil. Serve, garnished with peanuts.

Note: This soup is also good served ice cold.

BISQUE OF HAMPTON CRAB
(6 servings)

Hampton Roads, at the mouth of the James River, is the chief anchorage for the ports of Norfolk, Portsmouth, and Newport News, which surround it. At times, it is said, the Roads have been so crowded with cargo vessels that one could cross the waterway by walking from deck to deck, though there is no record of anyone trying it. Shellfish, among them crabs, flourished in abundance in earlier years along the bottom of Hampton Roads, unheeding of the bustle overhead.

1 cup crabmeat
1 can condensed cream of
   mushroom soup
1 can condensed cream of
   asparagus soup
1 cup light cream

1¼ cups milk
½ teaspoon Worcestershire
   sauce
⅛ teaspoon Tabasco sauce
⅓ cup dry sherry

Pick over the crabmeat and remove any bits of shell or cartilage.

Purée the crabmeat and soups in a food processor or a blender.

Pour into a saucepan, add the remaining ingredients, and heat just until hot, not boiling.

BISQUE OF CLAM AND CHICKEN

(4–6 servings)

1½ cups clam juice
2 tablespoons onion, finely
   chopped
¼ cup celery, diced
1 small bay leaf
2 cups CHICKEN STOCK *(page*
   45), or canned chicken
   broth
2 tablespoons butter
3 tablespoons all-purpose
   flour

1 cup cooked chicken, finely
   chopped
½ cup clams, finely chopped
1 cup light cream
salt and white pepper to taste
¼ cup whipping cream
1 tablespoon pimiento,
   drained and finely chopped

Simmer the clam juice with the onion, celery, and bay leaf for 30 minutes.

Add the Chicken Stock and bring to a boil.

Strain and discard the vegetables and bay leaf.

Melt the butter in a medium-sized saucepan and blend in the flour.

Add the hot stock all at once and stir vigorously until evenly blended.

Add the chicken, clams, light cream, and salt and pepper to taste.

Simmer 20 minutes over low heat, stirring occasionally, but do not boil.

Whip the cream until soft peaks form. Fold in the well-drained pimiento.

Serve the bisque in warm bowls. Top each serving with 1 tablespoon of the whipped cream-pimiento mixture.

Note: This bisque is very rich—servings should be small.

WILLIAMSBURG INN
CHILLED CRAB GUMBO
(12 servings)

Bouquet garni:

6 parsley stems, chopped	*pinch of saffron*
1 clove garlic, minced	*1 cup okra, chopped (see note)*
½ teaspoon leaf thyme	*1 cup tomatoes, chopped*
½ teaspoon leaf marjoram	*1 teaspoon salt or to taste*
2 bay leaves	*½ teaspoon white pepper*
½ cup celery, finely chopped	*½ teaspoon gumbo filé powder*
½ cup onion, finely chopped	*(see note)*
½ cup green pepper, finely chopped	*1 envelope unflavored gelatin softened in ½ cup cold water*
½ cup leeks, finely chopped	
1 pound crabmeat, cooked	*1 cup rice, cooked*

Prepare a bouquet garni by tying the herbs in a cheesecloth bag.

Heat 2 quarts of water to boiling and add the bouquet garni, celery, onion, green pepper, and leeks.

Cover and simmer 20 minutes.

Pick over the crabmeat and remove any bits of shell or cartilage.

Add the crabmeat and saffron to the simmering vegetables and continue to simmer slowly for 15 minutes.

Add the okra, tomatoes, salt, and pepper.

Remove ½ cup of the liquid from the pot, sprinkle in the filé powder, and beat thoroughly.

Stir into the pot. *Be careful not to let the soup boil after the filé powder has been added or it will become stringy and unfit to serve.*

Stir in the softened gelatin. Remove from the heat, add the cooked rice, and adjust the seasoning.

Refrigerate overnight if possible to bring out the flavor.

Serve in cold cups.

Note: If canned okra is used, the liquid should be added to the gumbo after the cooking process because it will enhance the flavor of the soup. If raw okra is used, blanch it in 2 cups of the stock before adding it to the gumbo.

Also note: Okra will take the place of filé powder if the latter is not available; however, gumbo tastes better when both okra and filé powder are used.

CHOWNING'S TAVERN BRUNSWICK STEW
(*8–10 servings*)

By all accounts, every place named Brunswick from Canada to the Carolinas has tried to claim this stew as its own. There have also been many arguments about what precisely went into the original pot, and what should go in now.

All in all, Brunswick County, Virginia, has the best claim to being the birthplace of this popular dish, which in its heyday was served at all of Virginia's tobacco-curings and public gatherings. The story goes that a hunting party in Brunswick County, well provisioned with tomatoes, onions, cabbage, butter beans, red pepper, bacon, salt, and corn, left one man behind to mind the commissary and to have dinner ready at day's end. Disgruntled, he shot a squirrel, the only thing he could find within range of the camp, and threw it into the pot along with the vegetables.

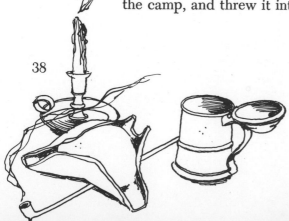

When it was served, everybody agreed that squirrel, one of the finest and tenderest of all wild meats, was what made the new stew just right. Chicken is now substituted.

*1 stewing hen (6 pounds), or
    2 broiler-fryers (3 pounds
    each)
2 large onions, sliced
2 cups okra, cut (optional)
4 cups fresh or 2 cans (1 pound
    each) tomatoes*

*2 cups lima beans
3 medium potatoes, diced
4 cups corn cut from cob or
    2 cans (1 pound each) corn
3 teaspoons salt
1 teaspoon pepper
1 tablespoon sugar*

Cut the chicken in pieces and simmer it in 3 quarts of water for a thin stew, or 2 quarts for a thick stew, until meat can easily be removed from the bones, about 2¼ hours.

Add the raw vegetables to the broth and simmer, uncovered, until the beans and potatoes are tender.

Stir occasionally to prevent scorching.

Add the chicken, boned and diced if desired, and the seasonings.

Note: If canned vegetables are used, include their juices and reduce water to 2 quarts for a thin stew, 1 quart for a thick stew.

Also note: Brunswick Stew is one of those delectable things that benefit from long, slow cooking. It is a rule in some tidewater homes never to eat Brunswick Stew the same day it is made, because its flavor improves if it is left to stand overnight and is reheated the next day.

OUTER BANKS CLAM CHOWDER
(6 servings)

Originally chowder was a fisherman's stew of French origin, with salt pork or bacon being as essential an ingredient as the fish. New Englanders probably got their early recipe for chowder from French settlers in Canada; Virginians got it more likely from the English, whose cookbooks contained recipes for "chouder, a sea dish." For some time now, corn and other ingredients have supplemented the fish, and chowderlike thick soups of meat and vegetables have also developed.

12 *large clams*
¼ *pound fat bacon* or *salt pork*
2 *medium onions, finely chopped*
3 *medium potatoes, cubed*

salt and white pepper to taste
2 *tablespoons cornmeal or*
  all-purpose flour
1 *cup light cream*

Scrub the clams and steam them in enough water to cover.

Remove the clams from their shells, chop fine, and reserve.

Strain the liquid and add enough water to make 6 cups. Reserve.

Cut the bacon in very small pieces or, if using salt pork, into ½-inch cubes.

Fry until crisp and brown.

Add the onions, potatoes, clams, and reserved liquid; simmer until the potatoes are done.

Season with salt and pepper.

Mix the cornmeal or flour with a little cold water and stir into the chowder.

Add the cream.

Serve at once in warm bowls.

Note: When fresh clams are not available, 2 bottles (8 ounces each) clam juice and 2 cans (7½ to 8 ounces each) minced clams and their liquid can be substituted.

CHESAPEAKE OYSTER BISQUE

(*8–10 servings*)

1 *quart oysters*
1 *bay leaf*
2 *medium onions, chopped*
  and divided
2 *ribs of celery, chopped and*
  divided
½ *cup butter*

¼ *cup all-purpose flour*
½ *teaspoon salt*
¼ *teaspoon white pepper*
1 *pint light cream*
¼ *cup dry sherry* (*optional*)
paprika or *parsley*

Drain and chop the oysters; reserve.

Add enough water to the drained oyster liquor to make 1 quart.

Add the bay leaf, 1 onion, and 1 rib of celery and simmer, uncovered, for 30 minutes.

Remove from the heat and allow to "ripen" at least an hour, then strain.

Melt the butter in a saucepan and add the remaining onion and celery. Sauté 5 minutes.

Stir in the flour but do not brown. Remove from the heat and add part of the oyster stock, stirring constantly.

Return to the heat and add the remaining stock, stirring until smooth.

Add the salt and pepper and simmer over low heat 10 minutes.

Add the oysters and cream; simmer gently 2 or 3 minutes.

Add the sherry, if desired, just before serving. Ladle the bisque into warm bowls.

Garnish with paprika or chopped parsley.

CREAM OF OYSTER AND SPINACH SOUP
(*12–16 servings*)

1½ *quarts oysters*
2 *pounds frozen chopped*
   spinach
6 *tablespoons butter*
⅔ *cup onion, coarsely chopped*
2 *ribs of celery, very finely*
   chopped
6 *tablespoons all-purpose flour*

½ *teaspoon garlic salt*
pinch of nutmeg
2 *tablespoons steak sauce*
salt and pepper to taste
1 *quart milk*
1 *quart light cream*
whipped cream

Cook the oysters in 3 cups of water until well done or firm; drain the liquid and keep it hot.

Purée the oysters in a food processor or a blender.

Cook the spinach until well done; drain well. Purée in a food processor or a blender.

Melt the butter over medium heat, add the onions and celery, and sauté, stirring constantly, until translucent.

Push the onions and celery to one side of the pan; sprinkle the flour over the butter and stir to make a paste.

Pour in the hot oyster liquid, whipping to make smooth. Simmer, uncovered, for 30 minutes. Strain.

Return to the heat and simmer.

Add the puréed oysters and spinach to the simmering liquid.

Add the garlic salt, nutmeg, steak sauce, and salt and pepper to taste.

Add the milk and cream and continue to simmer over low heat for 5 to 10 minutes, but do not boil.

Serve hot topped with whipped cream.

OYSTER STEW
(*4 servings*)

1 pint oysters	*dash of Tabasco sauce*
4 tablespoons butter, divided	*1 pint milk*
¾ teaspoon salt	*1 pint light cream*
pepper to taste	*paprika*

Drain the oysters and reserve the liquor.

Melt all but 2 teaspoons of the butter over medium heat and add the salt, pepper, and Tabasco sauce.

Add the oyster liquor to the butter and seasonings; stir to blend.

Add the oysters and cook only until the edges begin to curl.

Stir in the milk and cream and bring almost to the boiling point.

Serve in hot bowls, top with the remaining butter, and sprinkle with paprika.

CASCADES TURTLE GUMBO
(*12–15 servings*)

¼ cup vegetable oil	*1 tablespoon Worcestershire sauce*
2 cups onion, coarsely chopped	*pinch of cayenne pepper*
4 ribs of celery, cut in 1-inch pieces	*2 pounds turtle meat, coarsely chopped*
2 green peppers, coarsely chopped	*1½ cups okra, cooked (see note)*
1 clove garlic, minced	*1 cup long-grain rice, cooked*
1 gallon TURTLE STOCK *(page 43)*	*salt and pepper to taste*
1 bottle (8 ounces) clam juice	*1 teaspoon gumbo filé powder (see note)*
1 cup tomato purée	
2 cups whole plum tomatoes, chopped	

42

Heat the oil in a large pot.

Sauté the onion, celery, and green peppers until almost tender.

Add the garlic and cook 1 more minute, stirring constantly.

Add the Turtle Stock, clam juice, and tomato purée; bring to a boil, then reduce heat immediately.

Simmer 15 minutes, then add the tomatoes, Worcestershire sauce, cayenne pepper, and the turtle meat.

Simmer, uncovered, for 15 minutes.

Add the okra, rice, and salt and pepper to taste.

Remove ½ cup of stock, sprinkle with the filé powder, and beat until smooth.

Return to the pot and stir well, *but be careful not to let the stock boil after the filé powder has been added or it will become stringy and unfit to serve.*

Note: If canned okra is used, the liquid should be added to the gumbo after the cooking process because it will enhance the flavor of the soup. If raw okra is used, blanch it in 2 cups of the stock before adding it to the gumbo.

Also note: Okra will take the place of filé powder if the latter is not available; however, gumbo tastes better when both okra and filé powder are used.

TURTLE STOCK

(*1 gallon*)

2½ to 3 pounds turtle meat, tied in a cheesecloth
2 cups onion, chopped
3 ribs of celery, cut in 1-inch pieces
2 carrots, sliced
pinch of leaf thyme

1 bay leaf
6 peppercorns
6 cloves
2½ cups whole plum tomatoes with liquid
1 cup tomato purée

Combine all of the above ingredients with 1½ gallons of water in a large pot, and allow to come to a boil.

Reduce the heat and simmer, partially covered, approximately 1½ hours.

Check the turtle meat to see if it comes easily from the bones. If it does, remove it from the stock and reserve. If not, allow the stock to simmer a few more minutes.

Continue cooking the stock, uncovered, for 30 minutes.

Pick the turtle meat from the bones for use in gumbo.

Strain the stock through a cheesecloth.

WILLIAMSBURG LODGE CORN CHOWDER

(6 servings)

3 ounces salt pork, cubed
1 large onion, chopped
1 rib of celery, chopped
1½ cups potatoes, diced
2 cups CHICKEN STOCK (page 45), or canned chicken broth

2 cups cream-style corn
2 cups milk
¼ cup butter
salt and white pepper to taste

Fry the salt pork until brown.

Add the onion and sauté over medium heat 5 minutes, stirring often.

Add the celery, potatoes, Chicken Stock, and 1 cup of water and simmer until the potatoes are done.

Add the corn and simmer 5 minutes, stirring occasionally.

Heat the milk and butter and add to the soup.

Add salt and pepper to taste and serve hot.

BEEF STOCK

(4–5 quarts)

10 pounds beef bones (shanks or whatever is available)
¼ cup vegetable oil
3 medium onions, chopped
2 ribs of celery, chopped
2 carrots, chopped
2 cloves garlic, minced

1½ cups whole canned tomatoes
½ cup tomato purée
½ teaspoon leaf thyme
½ teaspoon black pepper
1 bay leaf

Preheat the oven to 400° F.

Saw the beef bones in half or ask the butcher to do it. Place them in a roasting pan and brown well in the oven at 400° F. approximately 45 minutes.

Remove from the oven, drain the fat, and place the bones in a large soup pot.

Heat the oil in a heavy skillet. Add the onion, celery, carrots, and garlic; brown well. Drain.

Add the browned vegetables, tomatoes, tomato purée, and seasonings to the pot of bones.

Cover with cold water and bring to a boil. Reduce the heat and simmer, uncovered, for 6 to 8 hours.

Strain the stock through a double thickness of cheesecloth.

Note: Stock can be frozen in cubes for future use.

CHICKEN STOCK
(4 quarts)

Bouquet garni:
  ½ teaspoon leaf thyme
  1 small bay leaf
  ½ teaspoon leaf marjoram
  3 sprigs parsley
  6 peppercorns
2 medium onions
3 to 4 ribs of celery with
  leaves

3 to 4 carrots, washed but
  not peeled
2 to 3 leeks or spring onions,
  including green tops
4 to 5 pounds chicken necks,
  backs, and wings
1 tablespoon salt
1 cup dry white wine
  (optional)

Prepare a bouquet garni by tying the herbs in a cheesecloth bag.

Cut the vegetables into 1-inch pieces.

Put all of the ingredients into a large soup pot with enough water to cover them by at least 2 inches.

Bring to a boil over medium heat. Partially cover and simmer for 2 to 3 hours, or until the chicken comes easily from the bones; remove the chicken.

Remove the cover and continue to simmer the stock over low heat until it is reduced to about 4 quarts.

Strain the stock, refrigerate, and, when cold, remove all fat.

Note: Stock can be frozen in cubes for future use.

Meats

S ince beef cattle roamed until they were lean and tough, veal and pork were the most popular domestic meats in eighteenth-century Virginia. Not until about the 1890s did grain-fed beef find wide acceptance in the diet of Virginians. Pork, and above all ham, held its favored place on the bills of fare over the centuries. Epicurean Virginians rarely mentioned ham in diaries because there was no Virginian of consequence who did not have ham on his table at all times, with other meats of course.

Beef is beef and pork is pork wherever they come from, but Virginia ham is about as different from most other hams as chalk is from cheese. Unlike the pinkish, soft meat of ordinary hams, the truly aged Virginia ham is of a rich mahogany color, firm, and highly flavored. To be served properly, it should be cut paper thin.

The pig of the early Tidewater, left to forage in the forests for its food, grew into a smaller and leaner hog than his pen-fed descendants. The half-wild porkers multiplied so rapidly that as early as 1639 ham and bacon were being shipped to England. Because of climate and the long voyage by sailing ship, proper curing was of prime importance. The slow smoking over smoldering hickory wood and the months of undisturbed aging gave the hams a distinctive flavor that rivaled Europe's best. Hugh Jones wrote in 1724, "The hams being scarce to be distinguished from those of Westphalia."

The curing and shipping of Virginia hams gradually became concentrated in the counties of Suffolk and Surry, south of the James River. Smithfield, which became the Virginia ham capital, was named not for London's famous meat market but for Arthur Smith, on whose land the town was founded in 1752. Luckily the soil, which was too poor for tobacco growing, proved ideal for growing peanuts, and peanuts are a crop that hogs relish.

Nowadays, instead of running wild in the forests, the hogs are turned loose to glean the vast peanut-growing acreages below the James River where ripe, unroasted peanuts remain after harvesting. The distinctive flavor that is produced by the combination of diet and cure has remained a favorite for generations. Britain's Queen Victoria had a regular order for the hams of the peanut-fed hogs. During her visit in 1957, Queen Elizabeth liked Virginia ham so well that her host, Winthrop Rockefeller, sent a ham to her in London.

VIRGINIA HAM
AND BRANDIED PEACHES

Williamsburg visitors who plan to carry home a Virginia ham as a souvenir are advised to heed these preliminary directions or they may be sadly disappointed:

Scrub the ham to remove the coating of seasonings; cover it with water and soak for 24 hours.

Place the ham, skin side down, in a pan with enough fresh water to cover; bring to a boil, then reduce heat and simmer, covered, for 20 to 25 minutes per pound.

When done, skin the ham and trim off excess fat.

Note: These directions apply to a Virginia ham that has been cured for at least 12 months. If the ham has been cured less than 12 months, follow instructions on the wrapper or hang the ham and allow it to age.

Virginia ham (10 to 12 pounds)
2 tablespoons light brown sugar
1 tablespoon bread crumbs
1 teaspoon ground cloves

3 tablespoons honey, dry sherry, or *sweet-pickle vinegar*
BRANDIED PEACHES *(page 48)*

Preheat the oven to 375° F.

Combine the brown sugar, bread crumbs, and cloves and press the mixture into the ham.

Place the ham in a shallow baking pan and bake at 375° F. for 15 minutes or until the sugar melts.

Remove from the oven and drizzle honey, sherry, or sweet-pickle vinegar on the ham.

Return to the oven for 15 minutes.

Serve, garnished with Brandied Peaches, spiced crab apples, or any spiced fruit.

BRANDIED PEACHES

(*1 quart*)

Sent to family or friends back home in England, a Virginia ham made a delectable and much appreciated gift. So did peach brandy. In a letter of 1758 to Theodorick Bland, Sr., of Virginia, the Liverpool merchant Charles Gore expressed his thanks for the "kind present of hams and peach brandy."

Another favorite was brandied peaches. St. George Tucker of Williamsburg, writing to his daughter in 1804, passed on a recipe for "Brandy Peaches." * In his fine, clear handwriting he advised her:

> "Peel your peaches & put them in a stone pot—set the pot into a vessel of water, and let it boil until a straw will pierce the fruit—Then make a syrup of brandy and sugar—1 lb. of sugar to a qt. of brandy. Set in your peaches—They will be fit for use in a month—Brown sugar will do very well—Better without peeling SGT."

Today you can prepare brandied peaches by a quicker method and thereby provide an excellent accompaniment to Virginia Ham.

2 cans (1 pound, 13 ounces each) peach halves	½ cup brandy, preferably a peach or fruit brandy
½ cup sugar	3 to 4 drops almond extract

* *Quoted by permission from the Tucker-Coleman Collection, Earl Gregg Swem Library, College of William and Mary in Virginia.*

Drain the peaches and reserve 1 cup of the juice.

Boil the reserved peach juice until it is reduced to ½ cup.

Add ½ cup of sugar and ½ cup of brandy to the juice. Mix well. Add the almond extract. Cool.

Pour the brandy syrup over the peaches and serve, or pack the peaches in a sterilized 1-quart glass jar, add the brandy syrup, and seal.

VIRGINIA HAM LOAF
(6 servings)

¾ *pound* Virginia Ham *(page 47), cooked and ground*
¾ *pound smoked ham, cooked and ground*
1 cup potatoes, mashed
2 eggs, well beaten
1 medium onion, finely chopped

¼ *cup bread crumbs*
2 tablespoons milk
½ *cup* Barbecue Sauce *(page 93), divided*
salt and pepper to taste
cloves (optional)

Preheat the oven to 350° F.

Grease an 8½ x 4½ x 2½-inch loaf pan or 6 individual loaf pans 4½ x 2½ x 1½ inches.

Mix the hams together well and blend in the mashed potatoes.

Stir in the eggs, onion, bread crumbs, and milk.

Mix in 2 tablespoons of Barbecue Sauce and salt and pepper to taste.

Turn into the prepared pan or pans and press down to avoid air pockets.

Insert several whole cloves if desired.

Spread the remaining Barbecue Sauce over the top.

Bake the large loaf at 350° F. for 50 to 60 minutes or the smaller loaves for 40 to 45 minutes.

CASCADES PORK TENDERLOIN BROCHETTE
(*4 servings*)

1 pound pork tenderloin
TERIYAKI SAUCE (*below*)
1 large green pepper
1 jar (10 ounces) kumquats

1 jar (11 ounces) preserved
  orange sections with rind
12 chunks canned pineapple

Place the pork and Teriyaki Sauce in a shallow dish and marinate overnight. Turn occasionally.

Prepare the grill so that the coals are light gray and hot when the brochettes are ready.

Trim off all fat, and cut the pork into 16 pieces 2½ inches square by ½ inch thick.

Cut the green pepper into 12 chunks.

Skewer the pork, kumquats, pepper chunks, orange slices, and pineapple chunks alternately, repeating until all 4 skewers hold 4 pieces of pork (beginning and ending with pork) and 3 kumquats, pepper chunks, orange slices, and pineapple chunks each.

Place on the grill 3 to 4 inches from hot coals; grill for 5 to 7 minutes.

Turn, baste with Teriyaki Sauce, and grill for an additional 5 to 7 minutes.

Continue basting and cooking for a total of 15 to 20 minutes or until the pork is well done, with no pink showing, and is browned on all sides.

Note: Saffron rice is an excellent accompaniment for this dish.

TERIYAKI SAUCE

¼ cup dry sherry
½ cup soy sauce
½ cup CHICKEN STOCK (*page 45*), or *canned chicken broth*

½ cup pineapple juice
1 teaspoon fresh ginger, grated

Heat the sherry to the boiling point.

Add the soy sauce, Chicken Stock, pineapple juice, and ginger.

Bring to a boil, remove from the heat, and allow to cool to room temperature before marinating the pork.

PORK CHOPS AND SWEET POTATOES
(*4 servings*)

3 to 4 medium sweet potatoes
4 center-cut pork chops
salt and pepper to taste
all-purpose flour
2 tablespoons shortening
2 tablespoons butter, melted
½ cup currant jelly

½ cup orange juice
1 tablespoon lemon juice
rind of 1 lemon, grated
1 teaspoon dry mustard
1 teaspoon paprika
½ teaspoon ground ginger

Preheat the oven to 350° F.

Boil and slice the sweet potatoes.

Salt and pepper the chops, dredge in flour, and brown on both sides in the shortening.

Melt the butter in a small saucepan. Stir in the jelly, juices, and lemon rind. Add the remaining ingredients, stirring to blend.

Arrange the sweet potatoes and chops in a shallow casserole and cover with ¾ cup of sauce.

Bake, uncovered, at 350° F. for 30 to 40 minutes, basting occasionally with the remaining sauce.

BEEFSTEAK AND KIDNEY PIE
(*5–6 servings*)

There are two versions of this old English favorite. Beefsteak and kidney pie is made with a light, short crust; beefsteak and kidney pudding with a light, suet crust. It seems that the pie was popular in the colonies and the pudding in England.

¾ pound top sirloin of beef,
   cut into 1-inch cubes
½ pound lamb, beef, or veal
   kidneys
¼ teaspoon salt
¼ teaspoon pepper
¼ teaspoon paprika
¼ cup all-purpose flour
1 medium onion, thinly sliced

2 tablespoons shortening
2 cups BEEF STOCK (page 44),
   or 2 cups beef bouillon
1 bay leaf
4 mushrooms, sliced
1 tablespoon butter
2 hard-cooked eggs, sliced
1 cup PASTRY CRUST MIX
   (page 133)

Preheat the oven to 450° F. 10 minutes before the pie is to go in.

Trim any fat or membrane from the beef and kidneys. Cut the kidneys into ⅛-inch-thick slices.

Place the salt, pepper, paprika, and flour in a paper bag and shake to mix. Add the beef, kidneys, and onion and shake until well coated.

Melt the shortening in a large skillet or dutch oven, let it get very hot, and add the beef, kidneys, and onions.

Sauté, stirring, over high heat until the meat is brown. Add the Beef Stock and bay leaf.

Reduce the heat to low, cover the skillet, and simmer 1 hour or until the beef is tender.

Remove from the heat and discard the bay leaf. Cool. Place in a 1½-quart baking dish.

Sauté the sliced mushrooms in the butter. Top the meat mixture with the mushrooms and the sliced eggs.

Moisten the Pastry Crust Mix with ice water, roll out, and cover the pie, sealing the sides of the casserole. Cut vents for the steam to escape.

Bake for 10 to 15 minutes at 450° F., then reduce the heat to 350° F. and bake for an additional 15 to 20 minutes or until the crust is golden brown.

GINGER BEEF

(*4 servings*)

2 onions, chopped	½ cup vegetable oil
1 clove garlic, minced	1 cup canned tomatoes,
1½ teaspoons turmeric	drained
4 teaspoons powdered ginger	1 can condensed onion soup
1½ teaspoons salt	hot cooked rice
1¼ pounds flank steak or chuck roast, cut in strips	

Combine the onions, garlic, turmeric, ginger, and salt with the beef and let stand for 1 hour.

Heat the oil in a heavy pan and sauté the beef mixture.

Add the tomatoes and onion soup.

Cover and simmer 1½ to 2 hours, adding a little water if the mixture seems too dry.

Serve with hot rice.

CASCADES BRAISED
SHORT RIBS OF BEEF
(4 servings)

¼ cup flour	½ cup celery, chopped
2 teaspoons salt	½ cup carrots, chopped
freshly ground black pepper	2 tablespoons shortening
¼ teaspoon powdered rosemary	2 cups BASIC BROWN SAUCE (page 94)
4 short ribs of beef	salt and pepper to taste
1 tablespoon butter	¼ cup red wine
½ cup onion, chopped	

Preheat the oven to 300° F.

Combine the flour, salt, freshly ground black pepper, and powdered rosemary. Dredge the short ribs in the seasoned flour.

In a heavy skillet heat 1 tablespoon of butter. Add the vegetables and sauté for 5 minutes. Transfer the vegetables to a heavy kettle with a lid.

Heat 2 tablespoons of shortening in the skillet. Brown the short ribs well on all sides and transfer them to the kettle.

Heat the Basic Brown Sauce just to boiling and add it to the kettle. Cover tightly.

Bake at 300° F. for 2½ hours or until the meat is very tender.

Skim off any excess fat. Strain the sauce and adjust the seasoning. If desired, the sauce can be thickened by adding a little flour mixed with cold water.

Just before serving, stir in the red wine.

KING'S ARMS TAVERN TENDERLOIN OF
BEEF STUFFED WITH OYSTERS
(4 servings)

4 7-ounce tenderloin steaks	4 slices bacon
12 medium oysters	1 teaspoon parsley, chopped, or fresh chives, snipped
salt and pepper to taste	
3 tablespoons butter, divided	

Insert a sharp knife into the side of each tenderloin steak and, with a short sawing motion, make a pocket. Be careful not to puncture the other side of the steak.

Season the oysters with salt and pepper and sauté in 1 tablespoon butter and some of the oyster liquor only until the edges begin to curl; drain.

Stuff each steak with three oysters, wrap with a slice of bacon, and secure it with a toothpick. Broil or sauté.

Heat the remaining butter until light brown, add the parsley or chives, and pour over the cooked steaks.

Note: If the steaks are being prepared in advance, drain and cool the oysters before stuffing them.

KING'S ARMS TAVERN
PAN FRIED RABBIT
(4 servings)

1 rabbit (2½ to 3 pounds)	2 cups BASIC BROWN SAUCE
salt and pepper to taste	(page 94)
¼ cup all-purpose flour	1 teaspoon brown sugar
2 tablespoons shortening	4 tablespoons port wine
1 tablespoon butter	2 teaspoons red currant jelly
1 medium onion, sliced	

Cut the rabbit into portions and place it in a saucepan in one layer.

Add enough water to cover the rabbit, bring to a boil, reduce the heat, and simmer, uncovered, for 20 to 30 minutes or until the rabbit is tender. Drain and let cool.

Season the rabbit with the salt and pepper and roll it in the flour.

Heat the shortening in a heavy skillet. Add the rabbit and brown it on all sides.

Melt the butter in a small skillet. Add the onion and sauté until it is golden brown. Reserve.

In a small saucepan bring 2 cups of Basic Brown Sauce to a boil. Stir in the brown sugar, port wine, and red currant jelly.

Pour the sauce over the rabbit and garnish with the sautéed onion.

VEAL BIRDS GARNISHED WITH FRESH MUSHROOMS AND ARTICHOKE BOTTOMS

(6 servings)

6 veal cutlets (6 ounces each),
  well-trimmed
2 cups onion, finely chopped
1 cup butter, divided
2 cups bread crumbs
½ cup seedless raisins
salt and pepper to taste
pinch of powdered thyme
¼ cup milk

¼ cup all-purpose flour
½ cup dry sherry
2 cups BASIC BROWN SAUCE
  (page 94)
1 pound fresh mushrooms,
  quartered
6 artichoke bottoms,
  quartered
¼ cup parsley, chopped

Cut the veal cutlets in half, place them between layers of wax paper, one at a time, and pound the cutlets thin with a mallet or the side of a heavy knife blade or cleaver.

Sauté the onion in ½ cup of butter, stirring so it does not brown.

Add the bread crumbs, raisins, salt, pepper, and thyme.

Remove from the heat, add the milk, and mix well.

Spoon 2 tablespoons of the mixture close to one edge of each flattened piece of veal, roll up, and fasten with a toothpick.

Season the meat with salt and pepper, roll lightly in the flour, and sauté in ¼ cup of butter.

When brown, remove the veal from the pan, drain the fat, add the sherry, and allow to boil a second or two.

Stir in the Brown Sauce, return the meat to the pan, and simmer over low heat, covered, for 20 to 30 minutes or until the veal is tender when pierced with a fork.

Sauté the mushrooms and artichokes in the remaining butter.

Place the veal birds on a heated platter, cover with the sauce, and garnish with the mushrooms, artichokes, and parsley.

PORK BARBECUE SANDWICHES

(6 servings)

1½ pounds cooked pork,   *6 large hamburger rolls,*
  thinly sliced   *warmed*
2 cups BARBECUE SAUCE   *dill pickle* or *coleslaw*
  (page 93)

Combine the sliced cooked pork with the Barbecue Sauce. Heat thoroughly.

Spoon about 4 ounces of the pork barbecue onto each roll, and garnish with a dill pickle or coleslaw.

Note: 1 heaping tablespoon of coleslaw may be placed on top of the pork barbecue in the bun.

KING'S ARMS TAVERN COLONIAL GAME PIE

(12–15 servings)

salt to taste   *1 cup currant jelly*
1 duck (4½ to 5 pounds)   *1½ pounds mushrooms,*
2 pounds rabbit   *quartered*
2½ pounds venison   *½ cup butter*
½ cup vegetable oil   *1 pound slab bacon, cut into*
2 cups port wine   *¼-inch cubes*
1½ quarts BASIC BROWN   *1 can (15½ ounces) pearl*
  SAUCE *(page 94)*   *onions*
1 tablespoon Worcestershire   PASTRY CRUST MIX *(page*
  sauce   *133)*
1 clove garlic, minced   *1 egg*
½ teaspoon pepper, freshly   *2 tablespoons milk*
  ground

Preheat the oven to 400° F.

Salt the cavity of the duck and place it on a rack in a shallow roasting pan, breast side up.

Bake for 30 minutes at 400° F., reduce the heat to 325° F., and bake until the duck tests done.

Simmer the rabbit in a small amount of water for 60 minutes or until tender.

Cut the venison into large cubes and sauté in the vegetable oil in a large skillet until well browned, stirring and turning as necessary.

Remove the venison and drain the oil from the skillet.

Add the port wine to the skillet and boil for 2 to 3 minutes, scraping up any brown particles.

Return the venison to the skillet and add the Brown Sauce. Simmer for 45 to 60 minutes, or until the venison is tender.

Cut the duck and rabbit in medium-sized pieces, and place in the skillet with the venison to keep warm.

Season with the Worcestershire sauce, garlic, pepper, and currant jelly.

Sauté the mushrooms in the butter until lightly browned.

Fry the bacon until crisp; drain.

Heat the onions and drain.

Divide the mixture into individual greased casserole dishes and garnish the top of each with mushrooms, bacon, and onions.

Cover with the pastry crust, trim the edges, and prick the tops to allow the steam to escape.

Beat the egg lightly with the milk to make an egg wash and brush the tops of the pastry with the mixture.

Bake in a 350° F. oven for 20 to 25 minutes or until the crust is golden brown.

Serve piping hot.

Poultry

Restauranteurs know that chicken, prepared one way or another, is the second most-ordered food. Chicken has held its place as first choice among poultry and wild fowl the centuries and the years around. Turkeys are traditionally reserved for special occasions.

Astonishing to Virginia's first settlers were the "infinities of wild Turkeyes" at large in the woods. Discovered by the Spaniards and introduced into Europe years earlier, the big bird was already domesticated and playing its part in England's Christmas fare a quarter of a century before Jamestown was founded. Housewives found that each wild bird had a finger's thickness of fat on its back, which was better and sweeter for cakemaking than the best butter. Today, game wardens seeking to restock the wild turkey for the benefit of hunters are faced with the problem of keeping the wild birds wild. They prefer the comforts of being tame.

A pair of Roast Ducks with Fruit Stuffing are displayed in the dining room of the Thomas Everard House, the platter garnished with orange wedges, fresh mushrooms, roast potatoes, and seedless grapes.

WILLIAMSBURG INN
BREAST OF TURKEY SUPREME
(*6 servings*)

Brillat-Savarin (1755–1826), a famous French gastronome, said in his book on the art of dining that the turkey is surely one of the noblest gifts that the Old World received from the New. Perhaps he remembered the day during his stay in America when he killed a wild turkey in Connecticut and afterward prepared it with his own hands. However that may be, Chef Fred Crawford of the Williamsburg Inn considered this version of Breast of Turkey Supreme, his own, to be one of his finest entrées.

½ *cup butter*
½ *cup all-purpose flour*
2 *cups hot* CHICKEN STOCK
   (*page 45*), *or canned*
   chicken broth
1 *teaspoon salt*
⅛ *teaspoon white pepper*

1 *cup milk*
1 *cup light cream*
1 *pound turkey breast, sliced*
   cooked rice or *noodles*
3 *tablespoons toasted*
   almonds, chopped

Melt the butter and add the flour, stirring until smooth.

Pour the hot Chicken Stock into the butter-flour mixture and stir until smooth.

Add the salt and pepper.

Heat the milk and cream in a saucepan.

Pour into the thickened Chicken Stock and cook over low heat for 10 minutes, stirring often.

Serve the sauce very hot over sliced turkey breast and steamed noodles or rice.

Top with the toasted almonds.

Seafood from the Chesapeake Bay is a specialty of Christiana Campbell's Tavern, one of George Washington's favorite places to dine when the House of Burgesses was in session. Arrayed here, with lobster on the sideboard, are (front row) Cascades Baked Stuffed Flounder, Christiana Campbell's Tavern Made Dish of Shrimp and Lobster, (second row) Hampton Crab Imperial, and Williamsburg Inn Cornmeal Batter Cakes with Crabmeat and Virginia Ham.

BAKED CHICKEN WITH ALMONDS

(4 servings)

1 broiler-fryer (2¾ pounds)
all-purpose flour
½ cup butter, divided
1 cup CHICKEN STOCK *(page 45), or canned chicken broth*

½ cup blanched almonds, sliced
¼ cup dry sherry
salt and pepper to taste
2 teaspoons cornstarch

Preheat the oven to 400° F.

Cut the broiler-fryer into four portions, dredge with flour, and place on a rack in a shallow roasting pan.

Brush with ¼ cup of melted butter and bake at 400° F. until browned, 25 to 35 minutes.

When the chicken is brown, remove the rack, place the chicken in the bottom of a pan that will just hold it, and add the Chicken Stock to a depth of ½ inch.

Cover and bake at 350° F. for 1 hour.

Meanwhile, sauté the almonds in the remaining ¼ cup of butter until golden brown. Dissolve the cornstarch in the sherry. Stir it into the sautéed nuts.

About 10 minutes before the end of the cooking time, remove the cover and spoon the almond mixture over the chicken. Season with the salt and pepper.

SHIELDS TAVERN SAMPLER
FRICASSEE OF CHICKEN

(6 servings)

½ to 1 teaspoon mace
½ to 1 teaspoon nutmeg
½ to 1 teaspoon ground cloves
pepper to taste
1 frying chicken (2½ to 3 pounds), boned and chopped, or 2 pounds boned chicken meat, chopped
¼ pound butter
3 egg yolks

¼ cup white wine
¼ to ½ teaspoon of 3 or 4 sweet herbs (parsley, marjoram, basil, thyme, tarragon)
½ cup chicken broth
½ cup chicken gravy
1 tablespoon vinegar
1 slice of lemon, minced
salt to taste

Combine the mace, nutmeg, cloves, and pepper.

Season the chicken with the spice mixture and fry in the butter.

Remove the chicken and pour off most of the butter, leaving approximately 1 tablespoon.

Beat the egg yolks. Add the wine and herbs and mix well. Heat the egg mixture in a frying pan over very low heat, stirring continuously to prevent the eggs from coagulating.

Add the broth and gravy to the egg mixture. Cook until the mixture begins to thicken. Add the chicken, vinegar, and lemon and cook slightly longer.

Add salt to taste.

Serve over rice or noodles.

SHIELDS TAVERN
CHICKEN WITH VIRGINIA APPLE DRESSING
(8 servings)

8 6-ounce whole chicken breasts, boned
seasoned salt
VIRGINIA APPLE DRESSING
  (below)

EGG WASH *(page 62)*
bread crumbs
butter

Preheat the oven to 350° F.

Season the chicken breasts on both sides with seasoned salt.

Pound the chicken with a tenderizer to flatten the meat and create an even surface.

Place Virginia Apple Dressing on each piece of meat and roll up.

Roll each breast in flour; dust off the excess. Dip each breast in the egg wash; then roll in the bread crumbs.

Sauté the chicken in hot butter until golden brown.

Bake at 350° F. for 40 to 45 minutes.

VIRGINIA APPLE DRESSING

½ cup water
2 teaspoons honey
3½ tablespoons butter or margarine
¼ cup raisins

4 cups fresh bread crumbs
1 cup canned apples, drained and chopped
1 teaspoon nutmeg

Boil the water.

Stir the honey, butter, and raisins into the boiling water. Remove from the heat immediately.

Let the mixture cool. The raisins will puff up.

Mix the bread crumbs, chopped apples, and nutmeg into the cooled water mixture.

EGG WASH

1 egg   *⅓ cup milk*

Whisk the ingredients together.

CHICKEN MAYONNAISE
(*10–12 servings*)

2 broiler-fryers (2 to 2½ pounds each)
1 onion
5 ribs of celery, divided
1 envelope unflavored gelatin
2 tablespoons lemon juice
salt and pepper to taste
¼ teaspoon leaf thyme

1 cup canned peas, drained
1½ cups mayonnaise
½ cup pecans, coarsely chopped
3 hard-cooked eggs, chopped
salad greens
¼ green pepper, cut in strips
1 pimiento pod

Grease a 10 x 13-inch pan.

Simmer the chicken, onion, and 1 rib of celery, chopped, in 1 quart of water until the chicken is done, about 2 hours.

Remove the chicken from the broth, discard the skin and bones, and cut the chicken into bite-sized pieces when cold.

Strain the stock. Sprinkle the gelatin over 1½ cups of the stock to soften, then place over low heat and stir until dissolved; cool.

Add the lemon juice, salt, pepper, and thyme.

When partially set, add 4 ribs of celery, chopped, and the chicken, peas, mayonnaise, pecans, and eggs.

Turn into the prepared pan and chill several hours until set, or overnight.

Run a knife around the edge and turn out onto a chilled platter or tray lined with salad greens.

Decorate with "tulips" made of green pepper and pimiento.

ROAST VIRGINIA QUAIL WITH GRAPE SAUCE AND PEACH GARNISH

4 quail
salt and pepper
6 tablespoons butter, divided
36 white seedless grapes, divided
4 strips salt pork, blanched
4 shallots, finely chopped
2 tablespoons cognac
1 tablespoon vegetable oil

¼ cup dry sherry
1 cup CHICKEN STOCK (page 45), or canned chicken broth
1½ teaspoons cornstarch
1 teaspoon lemon rind, grated
2 teaspoons lemon juice
4 peach halves, canned
guava jelly

Preheat the oven to 400° F.

Salt and pepper each cavity and stuff with ½ tablespoon of butter and 3 grapes.

Dry the outside of each breast with a paper towel, butter, tie with a strip of salt pork, and season with salt and pepper.

Place the quail on a rack in a shallow roasting pan over the shallots and sprinkle with the cognac.

Bake at 400° F. for 15 to 20 minutes, basting with 3 tablespoons of butter and 1 tablespoon of vegetable oil. Test for doneness.

When almost done, remove the salt pork, baste, and brown under the broiler. Remove to a heated serving platter.

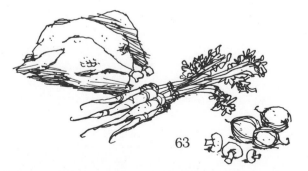

Heat the remaining grapes in the sherry and Chicken Stock. Remove the grapes and reserve.

Add the cornstarch to the sherry and stock mixture, stir in the grated lemon rind and lemon juice, and add to the pan juices and shallots.

Stir well, scraping up any brown bits on the bottom, and simmer until slightly thickened.

Remove from the heat, add the grapes, and pour the sauce over the quail.

Serve immediately, garnishing each quail with a peach half filled with guava jelly.

KING'S ARMS TAVERN CHICKEN POT PIE

2 broiler-fryers (2½ to 3 pounds each)
2 ribs of celery, chopped
1 medium onion, sliced
1 bay leaf
1 teaspoon salt
½ teaspoon white pepper
½ cup butter
½ cup all-purpose flour
1 package (10 ounces) frozen peas, cooked

4 ribs of celery, diced and cooked
4 carrots, sliced and cooked
1¾ cups potatoes, diced and cooked
1 egg
2 tablespoons milk
PASTRY CRUST MIX (page 133), as needed

Preheat the oven to 375° F. 10 minutes before the pies are to go in.

Grease 8 individual casseroles.

Put the chicken on to cook in a large saucepan with enough water to cover.

Add 2 ribs of celery, chopped, and the onion, bay leaf, salt, and pepper.

Bring the water to a boil, reduce the heat to simmer, and cook until the chicken is done.

Remove the fat and strain the stock.

Discard the skin and bones and cut the chicken into large pieces.

Melt the butter and stir in the flour.

Cook 5 minutes, stirring constantly. Add enough chicken stock, stirring constantly, to achieve the consistency of the sauce desired.

Simmer 5 minutes. Add salt and pepper to taste.

Divide the chicken and cooked vegetables equally into 8 individual casseroles.

Add the amount of sauce desired, gently lifting the chicken and vegetables so that the sauce will flow down and around.

Mix the egg and milk together to make an egg wash.

Cover each casserole with pastry, brush with the egg wash, and puncture the pastry with a fork in several places to allow the steam to escape.

Bake at 375° F. until the crust is golden brown. Serve piping hot.

WILLIAMSBURG INN
CHICKEN AND DUMPLINGS

1 stewing chicken (4 to 5
   pounds), or 2 broiler-fryers
   (3 pounds each)
1 small onion, sliced
1 carrot, sliced
2 ribs of celery with leaves,
   chopped
1 teaspoon salt

4 tablespoons butter or
   chicken fat
6 tablespoons flour
⅛ teaspoon paprika
½ cup light cream
white pepper to taste
DUMPLINGS (page 66)

Simmer the chicken, onion, carrot, celery, and salt in enough water to cover until the chicken is done, 1½ to 2 hours.

Remove the chicken from the broth. When it is cool enough to handle, remove the skin and bones and dice the chicken.

Strain the stock and, if necessary, add enough water to make 1 quart.

Melt the butter or chicken fat in a heavy saucepan.

Stir in the flour mixed with the paprika.

Add the chicken stock gradually, stirring constantly; cook for 2 minutes.

Add the chicken, cream, and pepper and adjust the seasoning to taste.

Spoon the Dumplings on top of the gently bubbling chicken mixture and cover. Cook for 15 minutes without lifting the lid.

Serve at once.

DUMPLINGS

2 cups all-purpose flour   *1 tablespoon shortening*
1 teaspoon salt   *¾ cup milk*
4 teaspoons baking powder

Sift the dry ingredients three times.

Blend in the shortening with a pastry blender or fork.

Add the milk and mix well.

Dip a teaspoon into cold water and then into the dough. Spoon the dumplings on top of the gently bubbling chicken mixture and cover. Cook for 15 minutes without lifting the lid.

Serve at once.

KING'S ARMS TAVERN
BONELESS BREAST OF CHICKEN
AND VIRGINIA HAM

⅓ cup all-purpose flour   *2 tablespoons vegetable oil*
⅓ cup fine cracker crumbs   *4 thin slices* VIRGINIA HAM
4 large chicken breasts, boned   *(page 47)*
salt and white pepper to taste   GRAPE SAUCE *(page 67)*
2 tablespoons butter

Combine the flour and cracker crumbs, season the chicken breasts with salt and white pepper, and roll them in the mixture.

Heat the butter and oil in a heavy skillet. Add the chicken breasts and sauté until golden brown.

Place each chicken breast on a thin slice of Virginia Ham, coat with the Grape Sauce, and serve immediately.

GRAPE SAUCE

1 cup CHICKEN STOCK *(page 45), or canned chicken broth*
½ cup orange juice
¾ cup seedless grapes

¼ cup raisins
¼ teaspoon sugar
⅛ teaspoon nutmeg
⅛ teaspoon cinnamon
1 tablespoon cornstarch

Combine the first 7 ingredients and bring to a boil. Thicken the sauce with the cornstarch dissolved in a little cold water.

ROAST DUCK
WITH FRUIT STUFFING
(4–6 servings)

The chances are that the roast duck on the menu nowadays is a domesticated bird. Duck hunters remember that the wild bird was the inspiration for a unique American folk art, the art of the decoy, which was first practiced by the Indians. Duck hunters also know that the canvasback is acknowledged superior in flavor to any other species of wild duck. Apparently the Indians thought so too.

Adele Earnest in *The Art of the Decoy* tells how archaeologists discovered the first known American Indian decoys, and notes that several were made out of native bulrushes and painted. The broad white saddle of feathers bound to the body, the wedge-shaped head, and the red sienna of head and neck made them instantly recognizable as canvasback ducks.

1 duck (5 to 6 pounds)
salt and pepper to taste
FRUIT STUFFING *(page 68)*
½ cup orange juice

seedless grapes
orange wedges
mushrooms
roast potatoes

Preheat the oven to 400° F.

Grease muffin tins for the stuffing.

Salt and pepper the inside of the duck and stuff lightly with Fruit Stuffing.

Place the duck, breast up, on a rack in a roasting pan and roast at 400° F. for 30 minutes.

Reduce the heat to 325° F. and bake until the duck tests done, brushing it frequently with the orange juice.

Place the remaining stuffing in the prepared muffin tins and bake for the last 30 minutes of the baking time.

If the duck browns too rapidly, cover it with a tent of aluminum foil.

If the duck appears to be fat, prick the skin with a fork occasionally during baking.

The duck tests done when the juices are no longer pink or the drumstick feels soft when pressed.

Duck is customarily served quartered or with half of a breast fillet and a drumstick or thigh for each person.

Garnish with seedless grapes, orange wedges, mushrooms, and roast potatoes.

FRUIT STUFFING

¼ cup butter
1 package (8 ounces)
* herb-seasoned dressing*
1 tablespoon orange rind,
* grated*

¼ cup seedless raisins or
* currants*
1 large apple, grated with skin
* on*

Heat the butter and 1 cup of water in a skillet.

Stir in the remaining ingredients and toss lightly.

Fish and Seafood

Water, and fish, are everywhere in tidewater Virginia. Besides the Atlantic Ocean and Chesapeake Bay, four great rivers reaching far inland, plus tributary rivers, creeks, and deep-water inlets make the area a maze of waterways.

Fish, both fresh and saltwater, and shellfish abound. At one time oysters existed in such incredible quantities that ships had to avoid whole banks of them; sturgeon attained a length of from nine to twelve feet. Those people who lived along a riverbank could spear fish at their door and scrape up shellfish by the bushel.

Angling is an art on which Englishmen—and Virginians—have always prided themselves. But as Robert Beverley, the first native Virginian to publish a history of the colony and an avid angler, had to admit, catching fish was hardly an art in Virginia: "I have set in the shade, at the Heads of the Rivers Angling, and spent as much time in taking the Fish off the Hook, as in waiting for their taking it."

CHOWNING'S TAVERN
SAUTÉED BACKFIN CRABMEAT
(*4 servings*)

1 pound backfin crabmeat
1 teaspoon lemon juice
1 tablespoon shallots, finely
  chopped

6 tablespoons butter
salt and pepper to taste
dash dry sherry or *brandy*

Pick over the crabmeat and discard any bits of shell or cartilage.

Sprinkle with the lemon juice and toss lightly.

Sauté the shallots in butter over low heat until golden.

Add the crabmeat and cook over low heat only until the crabmeat is hot; do not brown.

Season with salt and pepper and a dash of sherry or brandy.

Serve hot in individual heated ramekins or casseroles.

CRAB CAKES
(*9–12 three-inch cakes*)

1 pound regular crabmeat
2 tablespoons lemon juice
Medium Cream Sauce:
  1 tablespoon butter
  1 tablespoon all-purpose
    flour
  ½ cup milk
  salt to taste
3 eggs, divided
2 tablespoons mayonnaise

1 cup bread crumbs, divided
1 teaspoon salt
⅛ teaspoon white pepper
1 teaspoon dry mustard
2 teaspoons Worcestershire
  sauce
¼ cup milk
¼ cup all-purpose flour
1 teaspoon paprika
shortening for frying

Pick over the crabmeat and discard any bits of shell or cartilage.

Sprinkle the lemon juice over the crabmeat.

Make a medium cream sauce by melting the butter in a heavy saucepan over medium heat and stirring in the flour, milk, and salt to taste. Continue stirring until the mixture is smooth and thick.

70

Beat 2 eggs. Add the cream sauce, mayonnaise, ¼ cup of bread crumbs, and the seasonings to the eggs. Stir well.

Gently combine the crabmeat-egg mixture. Chill until firm enough to shape.

Shape into 9 to 12 three-inch patties, depending on the thickness desired.

Mix the remaining egg and ¼ cup of milk together.

Bread the cakes lightly by dipping them into the flour, the beaten egg mixture, and the remaining bread crumbs mixed with the paprika.

Fry in the shortening, turning once.

CRABMEAT MORNAY

(4 servings)

1 pound regular crabmeat	2 tablespoons butter
3 egg yolks	salt to taste
½ cup light cream	2 tablespoons whipping cream
2 cups hot BÉCHAMEL SAUCE (page 94), divided	2 tablespoons Parmesan cheese, grated

Preheat the oven to 350° F.

Grease a 1 to 1½-quart casserole or 4 individual ones.

Pick over the crabmeat and discard any bits of shell or cartilage.

Mix the egg yolks with the light cream.

Add the Béchamel Sauce (reserve 2 tablespoons for topping), butter, salt, and crabmeat.

Turn the mixture into the prepared casserole or casseroles.

Combine the remaining sauce with the whipping cream and spread over the top.

Sprinkle with the Parmesan cheese.

Bake at 400° F. for 50 minutes or until lightly browned and heated through.

Note: 4 tablespoons of mayonnaise can be substituted in place of the sauce-cream topping.

71

Recipes

CRABMEAT RAVIGOTE

(6 servings)

1 pound regular crabmeat
¼ cup tarragon vinegar
3 tablespoons pimiento,
  drained and chopped
2 tablespoons chives, snipped
2 tablespoons sweet pickle
  relish

⅔ cup mayonnaise, divided
salt and pepper to taste
cleaned crab shells or lettuce
capers
pimiento

Pick over the crabmeat and discard any bits of shell or cartilage; marinate in the vinegar 15 minutes.

Drain the crabmeat and add the chopped pimiento, chives, relish, ½ cup of mayonnaise, and salt and pepper to taste.

Divide the mixture evenly into 6 cleaned crab shells or crisp lettuce cups; shape into domes.

Spread with a thin coating of the remaining mayonnaise.

Sprinkle some well-drained capers over the top and garnish with the pimiento.

Serve very cold.

HAMPTON CRAB IMPERIAL

(6 servings)

1 pound backfin crabmeat
½ tablespoon pimiento,
  drained and chopped
½ tablespoon green pepper,
  chopped
1 tablespoon butter
Heavy Cream Sauce:
  4 tablespoons butter
  5 tablespoons all-purpose
    flour
  1 cup milk
  ½ teaspoon salt

1 egg yolk
¼ teaspoon dry mustard
1 rounded teaspoon capers,
  drained
1½ teaspoons Worcestershire
  sauce
salt and white pepper to taste
1 cup mayonnaise, divided
paprika

Preheat the oven to 375° F. 10 minutes before the crab is ready to go in.

72

Grease 6 individual shallow casseroles or cleaned crab shells.

Pick over the crabmeat and discard any bits of shell or cartilage. Refrigerate.

Sauté the pimiento and green pepper in 1 tablespoon of the butter.

Make a heavy cream sauce by melting 4 tablespoons of the butter in a heavy saucepan over medium heat and stirring in the flour, milk, and salt. Continue stirring until the mixture is smooth and thick.

Combine the sautéed vegetables, cream sauce, and other ingredients except the crabmeat, mayonnaise, and paprika.

Mix in ¾ cup of mayonnaise.

Fold in the crabmeat very gently so that the lumps do not break up.

Spoon into the greased casseroles or shells and spread some of the remaining mayonnaise on top of each serving.

Bake at 375° F. for 30 to 35 minutes or until golden brown.

Sprinkle with the paprika and serve at once.

WILLIAMSBURG INN CORNMEAL BATTER CAKES WITH CRABMEAT AND VIRGINIA HAM

2½ cups milk	2 tablespoons sugar
1 cup cornmeal	3 eggs
1 cup butter, melted	VIRGINIA HAM (page 47),
2⅔ cups all-purpose flour	thinly sliced
2 teaspoons baking powder	½ recipe CHOWNING'S
1 teaspoon baking soda	TAVERN SAUTÉED BACKFIN
1 teaspoon salt	CRABMEAT (page 70)

Heat the milk and 2 cups of water almost to boiling, add the cornmeal, and whip until smooth. Cool to room temperature.

Add the remaining ingredients, except the ham and crabmeat, and beat well with a wire whisk. The batter will be thin.

Cook on a lightly greased hot griddle, allowing ¼ cup of batter for each cake. Turn once when small bubbles appear on the surface.

Place a slice of Virginia Ham on each cake, and top with 1 to 2 tablespoons of the crabmeat. Serve the cakes flat, or roll them as you would a crêpe.

Note: The batter tends to thicken toward the last of the cakes. If this happens, add a small amount of water or milk to restore the original consistency.

Also note: Additional batter cakes can be frozen between squares of waxed paper for future use.

CASCADES FRIED FLOUNDER AMANDINE
(6 servings)

2 pounds fresh flounder fillets	*1 egg, beaten*
salt and pepper to taste	*¼ cup milk*
2 tablespoons lemon juice	*1 cup all-purpose flour*
¼ pound saltine crackers	*½ cup vegetable oil*
¾ cup almonds, sliced	*½ cup butter*

Divide the flounder into 6 portions and season them with salt, pepper, and lemon juice.

Coarsely crumble the crackers and mix with the almonds.

Beat the egg and milk together to make an egg wash.

Dredge the flounder in the flour and dip it into the egg wash.

Roll it in the cracker-almond mixture, patting down firmly so that the mixture will adhere.

Heat the oil and butter in a heavy skillet. Fry the fillets about 5 minutes on each side or until they are golden brown and flake easily when pricked with a fork.

Drain quickly on a paper towel and serve immediately.

A Cheese Soufflé fittingly presides over an assortment of egg and cheese dishes. Below it, clockwise, are Eggs Hunter's Style, Chowning's Tavern Welsh Rabbit, shad roe for a Christiana Campbell's Tavern Shad Roe Omelet, and Williamsburg Inn Fantasio Omelets.

CASCADES BAKED STUFFED FLOUNDER
(6 servings)

6 baby flounder, boned, or
   6 flounder fillets
SEAFOOD DRESSING(*below*)
salt and pepper to taste

3 tablespoons lemon juice
1 cup fine bread crumbs
¼ pound butter, melted

Preheat the oven to 375° F.

Grease a shallow baking pan.

Stuff each fish with 4 to 6 tablespoons of Seafood Dressing, or spread the same amount of dressing over each fillet. Roll, and fasten with toothpicks.

Place in the prepared baking pan and season with the salt, pepper, and lemon juice.

Sprinkle the bread crumbs over the fish.

Melt the butter and pour over the fish.

Bake at 375° F. for 25 to 30 minutes or until the fish flakes easily when tested with a fork.

SEAFOOD DRESSING

6 tablespoons butter
¼ cup celery, finely chopped
½ cup onion, finely chopped
¼ cup green pepper, finely
   chopped
½ pound shrimp, cooked and
   diced
1 teaspoon parsley, chopped
1 teaspoon pimiento, finely
   chopped

½ teaspoon paprika
1 teaspoon Worcestershire
   sauce
½ teaspoon seafood seasoning
salt to taste
⅛ teaspoon cayenne pepper
¼ cup dry sherry
1½ cups bread crumbs

Melt the butter, add the vegetables, and sauté until tender.

◀   *Salmagundi—the eighteenth-century English name for what is now known as chef's salad—is shown here in the kitchen of Wetherburn's Tavern, among slices of ham and ingredients fresh from the garden.*

Add all of the remaining ingredients except the bread crumbs to the vegetables and cook over low heat for 10 minutes.

Add this mixture to the bread crumbs and mix thoroughly.

SEAFOOD GUMBO

(8 servings)

Although people in other countries eat okra, gumbo is distinctively American. Originally a Louisiana concoction of seafood thickened and flavored with the young and tender pods of okra and with gumbo filé powder—powdered sassafras leaves—the dish spread throughout the South. "Gumbo" is the Negro expression for the okra plant, which grows prolifically in the South, and may be seen in the Wythe House garden in Williamsburg. By the early 1800s a Virginia hostess spoke of gumbo as "traditional" when she was a girl. By then, too, the choice of ingredients was wider: fowl or a knuckle of veal might have been used instead of fish.

1 pound medium shrimp, raw
celery tops
¼ cup celery, diced
¼ cup onion, diced
¼ cup green pepper, diced
1 small clove garlic, minced
¼ cup butter, divided
2 cups canned tomatoes
½ cup tomato purée
3 tablespoons all-purpose flour
½ cup scallops, quartered
½ cup okra, chopped (see note)

dash of Tabasco sauce
½ teaspoon Worcestershire
* sauce*
½ bay leaf
2 teaspoons salt
1½ teaspoons gumbo filé
* powder (see note)*
½ cup regular crabmeat
½ cup whole oysters
1 cup rice, cooked (optional)

Peel the shrimp, saving the hulls, and dice. Reserve.

Put the shrimp hulls and a few celery tops into 2 quarts of water and boil for 30 minutes; strain.

Sauté the celery, onion, green pepper, and garlic in 2 tablespoons of the butter until tender but not brown.

Add the tomatoes, tomato purée, and 1 quart of the strained stock to the sautéed vegetables.

Let simmer for 25 minutes.

Make a roux by melting 2 tablespoons of the butter and stirring in the flour. Mix thoroughly and cook 3 to 4 minutes but do not brown.

Stir the roux into the stock and simmer for 5 minutes.

Add the diced shrimp, scallops, okra, Tabasco sauce, Worcestershire sauce, bay leaf, and salt to the stock and simmer for 20 minutes. Remove the bay leaf.

Remove ½ cup of liquid from the pot, sprinkle the filé powder over it, and beat until smooth.

Return it to the stock and simmer for 5 minutes. *Be careful not to let the stock boil after the filé powder has been added or it will become stringy and unfit to serve.*

Remove from the heat and add the crabmeat and oysters.

Serve in soup plates or in a casserole with or without the rice.

Note: If canned okra is used, the liquid should be added to the gumbo after the cooking process because it will enhance the flavor of the soup. If raw okra is used, blanch it in 2 cups of the stock before adding with the seafood and seasonings.

Also note: Okra will take the place of filé powder if the latter is not available; however, gumbo tastes better when both okra and filé powder are used.

CHRISTIANA CAMPBELL'S TAVERN MADE DISH OF SHRIMP AND LOBSTER

(4–6 servings)

1½ green peppers, quartered
3 medium tomatoes
2 packages (6 ounces each)
  long grain and wild rice,
  mixed
½ pound fresh mushrooms,
  quartered
¼ pound butter, divided
¾ pound lobster, cooked and
  shelled

1 pound shrimp, cooked and
  cleaned
1 can (15½ ounces) pearl
  onions
¾ cup dry sherry
1 teaspoon lemon juice
Worcestershire sauce to taste
salt and white pepper to taste
parsley, chopped (optional)

Partially cook the green pepper in boiling water, remove, and cut the quarters in half. Reserve.

Scald the tomatoes in boiling water for 60 seconds, drain, remove the skin, and cut in half. Squeeze out and discard the tomato juice and seeds and cut each half into 4 pieces. Reserve.

Cook the rice according to package instructions.

Sauté the mushrooms quickly in a small amount of butter and reserve.

Cut the lobster into bite-sized pieces.

Melt the remaining butter over medium heat and sauté the lobster, shrimp, and onions.

Add the sherry, lemon juice, and seasonings.

Add the green pepper, tomato, and mushrooms and simmer over low heat, stirring gently, until heated through.

Arrange the seafood and vegetables in a heated serving dish with the rice.

Garnish with the chopped parsley if desired.

TRAVIS HOUSE OYSTERS
(6–8 servings)

Built in 1765, the Travis House was moved to the present site of the John Greenhow House and restored in 1930. From 1931 until 1951, Colonial Williamsburg operated a restaurant there. One of its specialties was this recipe developed by the cook, Mrs. Lena Richards. After being served Travis House Oysters one admirer wrote, "The oysters—ah yes the oysters— they want nothing they have everything."

½ cup butter
½ cup all-purpose flour
1½ teaspoons paprika
½ teaspoon salt
¼ teaspoon pepper
dash cayenne
½ clove garlic, minced
1 medium onion, chopped

½ medium green pepper,
  chopped
1 quart fresh oysters
1 tablespoon lemon juice
2 teaspoons Worcestershire
  sauce
¼ cup cracker crumbs

Preheat the oven to 400° F.

Grease a 2-quart casserole or 6 to 8 individual casseroles.

Melt the butter in a large skillet over medium heat.

Remove from the heat, add the flour, and stir until smooth.

Return to the heat and cook, stirring constantly, for 5 minutes or until light brown.

Add the paprika, salt, pepper, cayenne, garlic, onion, and green pepper.

Cook 3 to 5 minutes, stirring constantly.

Add the oysters and their liquor, lemon juice, and Worcestershire sauce. Stir well.

Pour into the prepared casserole or casseroles.

Sprinkle with the cracker crumbs.

Bake at 400° F. for 20 minutes.

KING'S ARMS TAVERN
POACHED FILLET OF FLOUNDER
IN CREOLE SAUCE

(4 servings)

2 tablespoons butter
1 green pepper, diced
2 ribs of celery, thinly sliced
1 medium onion, diced
1 clove garlic, minced
2 cups canned tomatoes,
  coarsely chopped
salt and pepper to taste

¼ teaspoon thyme
dash of cayenne
dash of cloves
dash of nutmeg
1 pound fresh flounder fillets
COURT BOUILLON (page 80)
steamed rice

Preheat the oven to 350° F. 10 minutes before the dish is ready to go in.

Melt the butter in a heavy saucepan. Add the green pepper, celery, onion, and garlic and sauté, stirring occasionally, for 10 minutes.

Stir in the tomatoes, salt and pepper, and spices and simmer, stirring occasionally, for 10 minutes.

Lightly butter an ovenproof baking dish.

Place the flounder fillets in the prepared dish in one layer. Cover with the Court Bouillon, heated just until simmering.

Place the dish on a rack in the bottom of the oven and simmer 5 to 8 minutes, or until the fish tests done when pierced by a fork. Drain.

Pour the Creole Sauce over the fish and serve with steamed rice.

COURT BOUILLON

½ rib of celery
2 sprigs of parsley
½ bay leaf
½ cup white wine
4 cups water or part water and
*   part bottled clam juice*

5 peppercorns
pinch of thyme
1 small onion, peeled and
*   quartered*
½ teaspoon salt

Combine all of the ingredients in a saucepan and simmer, uncovered, for 20 minutes.

Strain the court bouillon through a double thickness of cheese-cloth. Cool.

SEAFOOD PIE
(4 servings)

2 chicken bouillon cubes
½ pound scallops
12 oysters
½ pound firm white fish, diced
5 tablespoons butter
¼ cup onion, chopped
¼ cup celery, finely diced

5 tablespoons all-purpose flour
½ cup lobster, cooked and cut
*   into bite-sized pieces*
¼ cup dry sherry
salt and pepper to taste
PASTRY CRUST MIX for 10-inch
*   double crust pie (page 133)*

Preheat the oven to 375° F. 10 minutes before the pie is ready to go in.

Dissolve the chicken bouillon cubes in 2 cups of hot water and bring to a boil.

Cook the scallops, oysters, and fish in the chicken stock for 5 minutes or until the fish flakes easily when pierced with a fork.

Remove the seafood and strain the stock. Reserve.

Melt the butter in a small skillet over medium heat and sauté the onions and celery. Stir in the flour, add the stock, and cook, stirring, until thickened.

Add the scallops, oysters, fish, lobster, and sherry.

Season with the salt and pepper. Cool.

Line a 1-quart casserole or four individual 5-inch casseroles with the pastry.

Pour in the seafood and top with the pastry. Cut vents in the top so that the steam can escape.

Bake at 375° F. for 25 to 30 minutes or until the pastry is golden brown.

Eggs and Cheese

H ens' eggs are best eggs, and the best be those that be new," a
fourteenth-century cookbook advised. Of which no more need be
said. Of cheese much more.

Anglo-Saxon cheeses are sturdy, set firmly, and keep a long time.
French and Italian cheeses are, on the whole, more expressive. Since
the native cheese is usually the perfect complement to the native drink,
it follows that Anglo-Saxons like cider or beer with their country
cheeses; the French and the Italians drink wine with theirs. William
Byrd II of Virginia liked his bread and cheese with punch.

BASIC OMELET

(2 servings)

3 eggs	*1 teaspoon butter*
1 tablespoon light cream	*1 teaspoon vegetable oil*
salt and pepper to taste	

Beat the eggs and cream together until the mixture is light and foamy.

Add salt and pepper to taste.

Heat the butter and oil in an omelet pan over high heat; remove the pan from the heat.

Add the eggs and return to the heat.

When the eggs begin to set, lift the edges with a fork or spatula so that any uncooked egg will run to the bottom of the pan.

Shake the pan occasionally to prevent sticking.

When the egg mixture is completely set, roll the omelet onto a warm plate and serve at once.

WILLIAMSBURG LODGE
COUNTRY OMELET

(2–3 servings)

2 teaspoons butter, divided	*5 chicken livers*
1 teaspoon green pepper, finely chopped	*3 eggs*
	1 tablespoon light cream
1 teaspoon onion, finely chopped	*salt and pepper to taste*
	1 teaspoon vegetable oil

Melt 1 teaspoon of butter over medium heat in an omelet pan; add the green pepper and onion.

Sauté, stirring, until the onion is translucent; remove.

Sauté the chicken livers, then chop them coarsely.

Beat the eggs and cream together until the mixture is light and foamy.

Add salt and pepper to taste.

Heat the remaining butter and oil in the omelet pan over high heat; remove the pan from the heat.

Add the eggs and return to the heat.

Before the eggs begin to set, add the green pepper and onion.

When the eggs begin to set, lift the edges with a fork or spatula so that any uncooked egg will run to the bottom of the pan.

Shake the pan occasionally to prevent sticking.

When the egg mixture is completely set, add the chicken livers.

Fold the omelet over, roll it onto a warm plate, and serve at once.

CHRISTIANA CAMPBELL'S TAVERN SHAD ROE OMELET

(1–2 servings)

3 ounces shad roe	*¼ cup light cream*
salt and pepper to taste	*¼ cup fine bread crumbs*
2 eggs	*2 tablespoons butter*

Drop the shad roe into boiling salted water to cover and cook until the roe is firm (about 6 minutes).

Drain the roe, chop it coarsely, and season with the salt and pepper.

Beat the eggs, cream, and bread crumbs together until the mixture is light and foamy.

Add salt and pepper to taste.

Heat the butter in an omelet pan over high heat; remove the pan from the heat.

Add the eggs and return to the heat.

When the eggs begin to set, lift the edges with a fork or spatula so that any uncooked egg will run to the bottom of the pan.

Shake the pan occasionally to prevent sticking.

When the egg mixture is completely set, add the shad roe, fold the omelet over, roll it onto a warm plate, and serve at once.

WILLIAMSBURG INN FANTASIO OMELET
(2–3 servings)

1 medium apple
1 slice stale bread
¼ cup butter, divided
2 ounces sausage meat
1 teaspoon chopped walnuts
   or *pecans*

3 eggs
1 tablespoon light cream
salt and pepper to taste
¼ cup Cheddar cheese,
   shredded

Peel and dice the apple.

Trim the slice of bread and cut it into croutons. Fry the croutons until they are brown and crisp in 1 tablespoon of butter, turning to brown on all sides; reserve.

Crumble the sausage meat and sauté until cooked through; drain and reserve.

Sauté the apple in the sausage drippings and, when it is almost done, add the chopped walnuts or pecans.

Combine the croutons, sausage, apple, and nuts; hold.

Beat the eggs and cream together until the mixture is light and foamy.

Add salt and pepper to taste.

Heat the remaining butter in an omelet pan over high heat; remove the pan from the heat.

Add the eggs and return to the heat.

When the eggs begin to set, lift the edges with a fork or spatula so that any uncooked egg will run to the bottom of the pan.

Shake the pan occasionally to prevent sticking.

When the eggs are completely set, mound the apple mixture and the shredded cheese on half of the omelet; fold it, roll it onto a warm plate, and serve at once.

EGGS IN CHEESE SAUCE
(4–6 servings)

CHEESE SAUCE *(page 95)*
6 hard-cooked eggs, sliced
buttered toast

paprika
parsley, chopped

Prepare the Cheese Sauce.

Gently stir the sliced eggs into the hot sauce.

When the eggs are hot, spoon the mixture over hot buttered toast.

Garnish with a sprinkle of paprika and chopped parsley.

EGGS HUNTER'S STYLE
(*2 servings*)

1 tablespoon onion, chopped	*4 eggs*
3 tablespoons olive oil or	*salt and pepper to taste*
butter	*buttered toast*
4 chicken livers, quartered	*1 tomato, quartered*
1 tablespoon tomato paste	*parsley*
¼ cup dry white wine	

Sauté the onion in oil or butter for 5 minutes or until it is golden.

Add the chicken livers and sauté, stirring, for 3 or 4 minutes.

Blend the tomato paste with 4 tablespoons of warm water, stir into the chicken livers and onion, and simmer 5 minutes.

Add the wine and cook 3 minutes, stirring occasionally.

Break the eggs into the sauce, being careful not to break the yolks.

Cover the pan and cook over medium heat 3 minutes or until the whites are firm.

Season to taste, serve on the buttered toast, and garnish with the tomato quarters and parsley.

BAKED EGGS IN CASSEROLE
(*4 servings*)

5 ounces VIRGINIA HAM (*page 47*)*, thinly sliced*	*2 tablespoons bread crumbs*
6 hard-cooked eggs, sliced	*½ cup Swiss cheese, grated*
1½ cups BÉCHAMEL SAUCE (*page 94*)	*paprika*

Preheat the oven to 375° F.

Cut the ham into thin strips. Arrange a layer of ham in 4 individual ramekins or in a 1½-quart casserole. Top with the sliced eggs and the Béchamel Sauce.

Sprinkle lightly with the bread crumbs, Swiss cheese, and paprika.

Bake at 375° F. for 8 to 10 minutes for the individual ramekins and 12 to 15 minutes for the 1½-quart casserole, or until the cheese is bubbly and golden brown.

CHEESE SOUFFLÉ

(*4–6 servings*)

½ cup butter
½ cup all-purpose flour
2 cups milk
½ teaspoon salt
dash of Tabasco sauce or
  cayenne pepper

2 cups sharp Cheddar cheese,
  grated
6 eggs, separated
1½ teaspoons dry mustard

Preheat the oven to 375° F.

Grease a 2-quart soufflé dish. If an especially high soufflé is desired, tie a 2-inch collar of well-buttered paper around the top of the dish.

Melt the butter over medium heat in a double boiler or heavy saucepan.

Stir in the flour and cook for a minute, then gradually add the milk and stir constantly until the mixture is smooth and thickened.

Add the salt and Tabasco sauce or cayenne pepper.

Remove from the heat, add the cheese, and stir until the cheese is melted, returning to the heat if necessary.

Beat the egg yolks until they are light and fluffy and add, stirring constantly.

Add the mustard and allow to cool completely.

Beat the egg whites until they hold stiff peaks, then gently fold the cheese mixture into the egg whites.

Pour into the prepared dish and bake at 375° F. for 15 minutes, then reduce the heat to 300° F. and continue baking for 40 to 50 minutes.

Serve at once.

CHOWNING'S TAVERN
WELSH RABBIT WITH BEER
(4 servings)

Welsh rabbit, or rarebit, has nothing to do with rabbit, but it is indeed a rare bit. There are quite different versions of its origin. Although Welsh by name, the "rabbit" is traditionally Old English, made from Cheddar or a Cheddar-type cheese produced for centuries at Cheddar in the English West Country, quite a step away from the Welsh border.

In 1774 Mrs. Hannah Glasse, in her *Art of Cookery Made Plain and Easy*, advised: "Toast the Bread on both Sides, then toast the Cheese on one Side, lay it on the Toast, and with a hot Iron brown the other Side." Another English cookbook makes this instruction clearer: Once the cheese is poured over the hot buttered toast, "hold the red-hot fire shovel over it."

Welsh rabbit is a favorite snack at Chowning's Tavern, and beer is its proper accompaniment.

1 tablespoon butter	*1 teaspoon dry mustard*
1 pound sharp Cheddar cheese, grated	*½ teaspoon salt*
¾ cup beer, divided	*½ teaspoon Worcestershire sauce*
dash of cayenne pepper or Tabasco sauce	*1 egg, slightly beaten*
	1 teaspoon cornstarch

Melt the butter in the top of a double boiler.

Add the cheese and all but 1 tablespoon of beer.

Cook over hot, not boiling, water until the cheese melts.

Combine the seasonings with the remaining tablespoon of beer and stir into the cheese.

Combine the slightly beaten egg with the cornstarch; stir into the cheese mixture and let it thicken slightly.

Serve immediately over toast or broiled tomato halves.

Salads

In Elizabethan England, fresh salad was always the first dish served at the five o'clock supper. England's John Evelyn wrote a discourse on *Sallets* in 1699 and listed some seventy-three kinds of *Esculents*. He advised that the greens be washed and drained in a "Cullender," and then swung in a clean napkin. After discreet choice of a mixture of olive oil, wine vinegar, salt, and pepper, with a touch of sugar according to taste, he wrote, "Composition is perfect."

Salads

CHRISTIANA CAMPBELL'S TAVERN
SALMAGUNDI

(8 servings)

Salmagundi was eighteenth-century England's name for what today is generally known in the United States as chef's salad. In present-day England, and in Colonial Williamsburg, the name has been revived. In colonial times salmagundi was served as a second course, or for supper.

salad greens (Boston lettuce, romaine, endive, watercress, and others, enough to serve 8)
1 pound VIRGINIA HAM *(page 47), thinly sliced and cut into strips*
1 pound turkey or *chicken, thinly sliced and cut into strips*
1 pound Cheddar cheese, thinly sliced and cut into strips
4 hard-cooked eggs, sliced
8 celery hearts
16 black olives
16 anchovy fillets
OIL AND VINEGAR DRESSING *(page 96)*

Arrange the greens on individual salad plates or on a large platter.

Place the remaining ingredients evenly over the top and around the greens.

Sprinkle lightly with Oil and Vinegar Dressing (page 96).

WILLIAMSBURG LODGE
CRABMEAT SALAD

(4 servings)

1 pound backfin crabmeat
1 cup celery, diced
⅓ cup mayonnaise
1 tablespoon lemon juice
½ teaspoon salt
dash of white pepper
few drops of Tabasco sauce
¼ teaspoon Worcestershire sauce
2 tablespoons FRENCH DRESSING *(page 95)*
lettuce

Pick over the crabmeat and discard any bits of shell or cartilage.

Combine the crabmeat and celery.

Mix the remaining ingredients together (except lettuce) and pour over the crabmeat.

Mix gently to avoid breaking the lumps of crabmeat.

Serve on lettuce.

SHIELDS TAVERN
CHILLED TURKEY SALAD
(6–8 servings)

3 pounds cooked turkey, diced
½ cup celery, finely chopped
¾ cup mayonnaise
½ cup French dressing
*2 tablespoons fresh lemon
    juice*
¼ teaspoon Tabasco sauce
*3 tablespoons onions, finely
    chopped*
salt and pepper

Combine the turkey and celery.

Add the mayonnaise, French dressing, and lemon juice. Mix well.

Add the Tabasco sauce and onions. Mix.

Add salt and pepper to taste.

Serve on a bed of lettuce with hard-cooked eggs, spring onions, orange sections, seedless grapes, and chopped nuts.

AVOCADO SALAD RING
(5–6 servings)

1 envelope unflavored gelatin
*2 tablespoons lemon juice,
    divided*
*1 heaping cup avocado,
    mashed*
½ cup sour cream
½ cup mayonnaise
salt and pepper to taste
dash cayenne or *to taste*
salad greens
fresh tomatoes or *fresh
    shrimp*

Lightly oil a 1½-quart ring mold.

Soften the gelatin in ¼ cup of cold water, add 1 cup of boiling water and 1 tablespoon of lemon juice, and stir until dissolved.

Chill until slightly thickened.

Purée the avocado in a food processor or blender.

Blend the sour cream with the mayonnaise and add to the avocado alternately with the remaining lemon juice.

Add the seasonings to taste and combine with the gelatin.

Pour into the prepared ring mold and chill until firm.

Unmold onto a serving dish covered with greens. Fill the center with diced fresh tomatoes or fresh shrimp.

CHRISTIANA CAMPBELL'S TAVERN CABBAGE SLAW

(8 servings)

1 large (2–2½ pounds) head firm cabbage	*½ cup cider vinegar*
1 tablespoon red pepper, diced	*½ cup vegetable oil*
	2 teaspoons sugar
	1½ teaspoons salt
1 tablespoon green pepper, diced	*¼ teaspoon white pepper*
	¼ teaspoon celery seed

Remove the hard core from the cabbage head and discard it. Shred the cabbage.

Add the diced red and green pepper.

Combine the vinegar, oil, and seasonings and pour over the cabbage. Toss lightly.

Dressings and Sauces

As one eighteenth-century English cookbook put it, the common or everyday sauces—butter, bread, egg, celery, onion, mushroom, and white sauces as well as gravy—belong to "the Rudiments of Cookery."

Sauces, for the most part, sound misguidingly simple to make. For that reason they are all the easier to spoil. Unless the first stage in the making of a sauce is just right, nothing can make the finished product good.

Mrs. Mary Randolph, in her day reputed to be the best cook in Richmond, wrote the first printed southern cookbook, *The Virginia Housewife* (1824). In prefacing her instructions for melting butter as a first step in making butter sauce, she warned, "Nothing is more simple than this process, and nothing so generally done badly."

There were other sauces, then as now, that accompanied certain dishes: applesauce for goose, mint sauce for lamb, and various fish sauces for fish. In Virginia, shellfish were used freely, especially the large and succulent oysters that were so abundant. Landon Carter of Sabine Hall would harvest twenty bushels at a time, some reserved "for Sauces of all kinds."

Now as then, a good sauce can make a poor dish passable, a passable one good, and beyond that the heights to which a sauce may ascend depend solely on the saucemaker's art. Saucemaking has often paved the way to culinary fame. The truly imaginative *saucier* can compound an infinity of sauces from a mere handful of foundation sauces by adding a pinch of this and a touch of that, in varying degrees.

ALMOND BUTTER SAUCE

(¾ cup)

2 tablespoons slivered almonds
½ cup butter, divided
2 tablespoons pimiento, drained
  and finely chopped

2 teaspoons parsley, finely
  chopped
2 teaspoons lemon juice
1 teaspoon salt

Sauté the almonds slowly in 2 tablespoons of butter until golden brown. Cool.

Cream the remaining butter and add the almonds, pimiento, parsley, lemon juice, and salt; mix thoroughly.

Serve with fried or broiled seafoods.

Note: If fresh parsley is not available, 1 teaspoon of dried parsley leaves can be reconstituted in the lemon juice before adding to the butter mixture.

Also note: This sauce can be stored in the refrigerator for 2 weeks.

BARBECUE SAUCE

(2½ cups)

1 cup onion, finely chopped
1 clove garlic, minced
¼ cup butter, melted
1 cup catsup
½ cup dry sherry
1 tablespoon light brown sugar

1 teaspoon dry mustard
1 tablespoon lemon juice
½ cup white vinegar
2 teaspoons Worcestershire
  sauce

In a deep saucepan sauté the onion and garlic in the melted butter for 3 to 4 minutes.

Add the remaining ingredients and ⅓ cup of water and bring to a boil.

Lower the heat and simmer, uncovered, for 1 hour, stirring frequently to prevent scorching.

Strain through a fine sieve.

BASIC BROWN SAUCE

(1½ quarts)

¼ cup butter
1 cup all-purpose flour
½ cup tomato purée
2 quarts hot BEEF STOCK
  (page 44)
1 tablespoon powdered beef
  bouillon

1 tablespoon bottled brown
  gravy sauce
salt to taste
caramel color (optional)

Melt the butter in a large heavy saucepan over low heat. Gradually add the flour and stir constantly until the mixture is chestnut brown. It may be necessary to turn off the heat completely at intervals so that the flour will not burn or become too dark.

When the desired color has been reached, add the tomato purée and stir well.

Gradually add the hot stock and powdered beef bouillon, using a wire whisk to insure smoothness.

Bring the mixture to a boil, then reduce the heat to the lowest degree possible.

Simmer 2 hours or until the sauce has been reduced to about 1½ quarts.

Add the bottled brown gravy sauce, salt, and caramel color if desired.

Remove from the heat and strain through a fine sieve.

Cool to room temperature and refrigerate.

BÉCHAMEL SAUCE

(2¼ cups)

4 tablespoons butter
1 small onion, grated
4 tablespoons all-purpose flour

2 cups hot milk or 1 cup hot
  milk and 1 cup hot CHICKEN
  STOCK *(page 45)*
¼ teaspoon salt

Heat the butter and onion together but do not brown.
Stir in the flour and remove from the heat.

Add the hot milk or milk and chicken stock mixture and the salt and continue to stir rapidly until the sauce is smooth.

Return to the heat and stir continuously until the sauce comes to a boil. Gently simmer and stir 3 to 5 minutes longer.

Strain through a fine sieve.

CHEESE SAUCE

(*2 cups*)

2 tablespoons butter
1 teaspoon onion, finely grated
2 tablespoons all-purpose flour
1½ cups light cream
¾ cup Cheddar cheese, grated

dash of Worcestershire sauce
pinch of cayenne
½ teaspoon paprika
salt to taste

Melt the butter over medium heat, add the onion, and cook only until the onion is golden.

Stir in the flour and add the cream to make a cream sauce.

Add the cheese and remaining seasonings and stir only until the cheese is melted.

Note: This is excellent served as a spread, or in place of hollandaise sauce on vegetables.

FRENCH DRESSING

(*1 cup*)

1 teaspoon salt
½ teaspoon black pepper,
   freshly ground
¾ teaspoon dry mustard

¼ cup wine vinegar
6 tablespoons olive oil
6 tablespoons vegetable oil

Mix the dry ingredients in a jar. Add the vinegar, cover, and allow to steep a few minutes.

Beat with a small wire whisk or fork while gradually adding the oils.

Cover and use at room temperature.

GARLIC FRENCH DRESSING
(1 cup)

Follow the instructions for French Dressing (page 95).
Add 1 small clove of garlic, crushed, to the dry ingredients and vinegar.

ROQUEFORT FRENCH DRESSING
(1 cup)

Follow the instructions for French Dressing (page 95).
After beating in the oils, add ¼ cup of crumbled Roquefort cheese and ¼ teaspoon of onion juice.
Shake gently to mix.

OIL AND VINEGAR DRESSING
(1 pint)

1½ teaspoons salt	*½ cup cider vinegar*
¾ teaspoon white pepper	*1½ cups vegetable oil*

Dissolve the salt and pepper in the vinegar.
Add the vegetable oil and shake vigorously in a covered jar.

WILLIAMSBURG INN HONEY DRESSING
(1¾ cups)

½ cup vinegar	*1 teaspoon celery seed*
¼ cup sugar	*1 teaspoon celery salt*
¼ cup honey	*1 teaspoon onion juice*
1 teaspoon dry mustard	*1 cup vegetable oil*
1 teaspoon paprika	

Mix the vinegar, sugar, honey, mustard, and paprika together, boil 3 minutes, and cool.

Add the celery seed and salt, onion juice, and vegetable oil and beat or shake vigorously.

Serve with any fruit salad.

If kept under refrigeration, shake well before using.

CASCADES PEPPER DRESSING

(1 cup)

1 cup mayonnaise
¼ teaspoon dry mustard
¼ teaspoon sugar
½ teaspoon salt
¼ teaspoon garlic powder
1 tablespoon Parmesan cheese, grated
1 tablespoon pepper, freshly ground

½ teaspoon lemon juice
¼ teaspoon Worcestershire sauce
¼ teaspoon bottled steak sauce
2 tablespoons water
dash of Tabasco sauce

Blend the ingredients together, mixing by hand.
Refrigerate before serving.

RUM BUTTER SAUCE

(3 cups)

1 cup sugar
2 tablespoons cornstarch
½ cup lemon juice
rind of 1 lemon, grated
½ cup butter

2 tablespoons brandy
¼ teaspoon nutmeg
½ cup light rum
2 tablespoons dark rum

Blend the sugar and cornstarch in 1 cup of boiling water.

Cook, stirring constantly, over medium heat until the mixture begins to thicken.

Add the remaining ingredients and cook for 2 minutes, stirring constantly.

Serve hot over mince pie, pound cake, or pudding.

WILLIAMSBURG INN REGENCY DRESSING
(*3 cups*)

1 tablespoon all-purpose flour
2 cups CHICKEN STOCK (*page 45*)*, divided*
1 tablespoon onion, finely chopped
1 clove garlic

½ cup vegetable oil, divided
2 tablespoons French-style prepared mustard
salt and pepper to taste
½ cup vinegar
1 egg yolk, lightly beaten

Mix the flour thoroughly with ½ cup of Chicken Stock.

Bring the remaining 1½ cups of Chicken Stock to a boil and stir in the flour mixture.

Cook for 5 minutes over medium heat, stirring constantly; remove from the heat.

Purée the onion and garlic in ¼ cup of vegetable oil in a food processor or blender; transfer to a mixing bowl.

Add the seasonings, vinegar, and egg yolk and mix.

Add the remaining oil very slowly, beating constantly.

Add the hot stock while continuing to beat.

Cool to room temperature before refrigerating.

Note: This dressing goes exceptionally well with hearts of Boston lettuce, watercress, or endive, or with any combination of fresh vegetables.

Vegetables

During his presidency, when he had little time to garden, Thomas Jefferson kept an account showing the earliest and latest appearance of each vegetable on the Washington market. He noted thirty-seven varieties of garden produce. New varieties of beans and peas—including black-eyed peas—pumpkins and squash, sweet potatoes and yams, plus all the culinary plants that grew in England, gave early Virginians a greater variety of vegetables than any other people had at that time.

Corn was the single most important vegetable for both the Indians and the colonists. Dried and ground it became meal, used in making bread. Possibly the favorite way of serving corn—then as now—was on the cob. As Virginia historian Robert Beverley described it in 1705:

> They [the Indians] delight much to feed on Roasting-ears; that is, the *Indian* corn, gathered green and milky, before it is grown to its full bigness, and roasted before the Fire, in the Ear . . . And indeed this is a very sweet and pleasing food.

CORN PUDDING
(*6 servings*)

3 eggs
2 cups whole kernel corn,
    well drained
1½ tablespoons sugar
½ teaspoon salt

1 cup dry bread crumbs
2 tablespoons butter, melted
2 cups milk
½ cup light cream

Preheat the oven to 350° F.

Grease a 1½-quart casserole.

Beat the eggs until they are light and fluffy.

Stir in the corn, sugar, salt, bread crumbs, and butter.

Add the milk and cream and mix well.

Pour into the prepared casserole and place the dish in a pan of boiling water.

Bake at 350° F. for 50 to 60 minutes or until the custard is set.

CORN PUFFS
(*12 puffs*)

1 egg, separated
⅓ cup milk
1 tablespoon butter, melted
½ cup cream-style corn

1 cup sifted all-purpose flour
1½ teaspoons baking powder
1 teaspoon salt

Beat the egg yolk. Add the milk, butter, corn, and sifted dry ingredients.

Beat the egg white until stiff peaks form; fold in.

Drop by tablespoonsful into deep hot fat or oil (375°) and fry until brown, about 3 minutes, turning once.

SHIELDS TAVERN SAMPLER
INDIAN MEAL PUDDING
(8 servings)

½ cup white cornmeal	*½ cup sugar*
1½ cups water	*¼ cup white wine*
¼ pound butter	*1 teaspoon nutmeg*
1 egg	*½ teaspoon mace*
3 egg yolks	

Preheat the oven to 400° F.

Grease an 8-inch square glass baking dish.

Make a cornmeal mush. Combine the cornmeal with the water. Bring the mixture to a boil, stirring continuously. Reduce to low heat and cook the mixture for 20 to 30 minutes, stirring continuously until the mixture thickens.

Mix the butter into the warm mush to melt the butter.

Combine and beat the egg and the egg yolks until they are light and fluffy.

Add the sugar to the eggs and beat until thickened.

Mix the egg mixture into the mush. Add the wine, nutmeg, and mace. Mix well.

Pour into the prepared baking dish.

Lower the oven temperature to 350° F. Bake for 30 to 40 minutes.

Serve hot or warm.

Note: This adaptation is quite sweet. You may wish to decrease the sugar to ⅓ cup.

CARROT PUDDING
(10–12 servings)

3 eggs, separated	*1 teaspoon salt*
4 tablespoons sugar	*1 cup fine bread crumbs*
1½ tablespoons cornstarch	*1 cup light cream*
1 cup milk	*½ teaspoon fresh nutmeg,*
3 cups (2 pounds) carrots,	*grated*
cooked and mashed	*¼ cup cream sherry*
3 tablespoons butter	

Preheat the oven to 300° F.

Grease a 2-quart casserole.

Beat the egg yolks and sugar until they are light and fluffy; hold.

Mix the cornstarch with a small amount of milk.

Heat the remaining milk, add the cornstarch, and stir until the mixture is smooth and slightly thickened.

Stir a small amount of the hot cornstarch mixture into the egg yolks and sugar.

Stir to mix well, then pour the yolks mixture into the hot milk and cornstarch. Cook, stirring, over medium heat until the mixture is smooth and thick.

Add the carrots, butter, salt, and bread crumbs; blend evenly.

Stir in the cream and add the nutmeg and sherry; mix well.

Beat the egg whites until they hold firm peaks; fold them into the carrot mixture.

Pour into the prepared casserole.

Place the casserole in a pan of hot water and bake at 300° F. for 30 minutes.

Increase the heat to 350° F. and bake for an additional 45 minutes or until a knife inserted in the center comes out clean.

SHIELDS TAVERN SAMPLER
CARROT PUFFS
(4–6 servings)

1 pound carrots, peeled and sliced	*1 teaspoon orange flower water*
1 egg	*3 tablespoons sugar*
2 egg yolks	*¼ cup dry sherry*
1 cup bread crumbs	*¼ cup heavy cream*
1 teaspoon nutmeg, freshly grated	

Cook the carrots until very soft. Drain well. Mash to a pulp.

Combine and beat the egg and egg yolks.

Mix the carrots, eggs, and remaining ingredients together thoroughly.

Gently drop by heaping tablespoonsful into deep hot shortening (375° to 400° F.) and fry until brown.

Place the puffs on paper towels to drain.

Serve immediately.

KING'S ARMS TAVERN
CREAMED CELERY WITH PECANS
(6 servings)

4 cups celery, cut diagonally
  in ½-inch pieces
2 tablespoons butter
2 tablespoons all-purpose flour

2 cups milk
1 teaspoon salt
¾ cup pecan halves
buttered bread crumbs

Preheat the oven to 400° F.

Grease a 1½-quart casserole.

Boil the celery in enough water to cover until tender; drain.

Melt the butter over medium heat; stir in the flour and slowly add the milk to make a cream sauce, stirring until thick and smooth.

Add the salt and well-drained celery.

Spoon into the prepared casserole, top with the pecans, and cover with buttered bread crumbs.

Bake at 400° F. for 15 minutes.

KING'S ARMS TAVERN
CREAMED ONIONS WITH PEANUTS
(4–5 servings)

16 whole small white onions
2 tablespoons butter
2 tablespoons all-purpose flour
¼ teaspoon salt
2 cups milk

¼ cup whole salted peanuts
½ cup buttered bread crumbs
¼ cup salted peanuts, coarsely
  chopped

Preheat the oven to 400° F.

Grease a 1-quart casserole.

Cook the onions in boiling salted water until tender; drain.

Melt the butter over medium heat; stir in the flour and salt.

Add the milk and cook over medium heat, stirring constantly, until smooth and slightly thickened.

Put the onions in the prepared casserole and pour the cream sauce over them.

Stir in ¼ cup of whole peanuts.
Top with the buttered crumbs and chopped peanuts.
Bake at 400° F. for 15 minutes or until the casserole is bubbly and lightly browned.

KING'S ARMS TAVERN
SWEET POTATOES
(8–10 servings)

3 pounds sweet potatoes
¾ cup light brown sugar,
   packed, divided
3 tablespoons butter

½ teaspoon cinnamon
½ teaspoon nutmeg
¼ teaspoon salt
1 cup milk

Preheat the oven to 400° F.
Grease a 1½-quart casserole.
Cook the sweet potatoes in boiling salted water until done; drain, peel, and mash them.
Stir in all of the remaining ingredients except 2 tablespoons of sugar.
Turn the mixture into the prepared casserole and sprinkle with the remaining sugar.
Bake at 400° F. for 30 minutes.

CREAMED SALSIFY OR OYSTER PLANT
(4 servings)

John Randolph of Williamsburg, the last king's attorney for the colony, wrote a *Treatise on Gardening*. It was the first kitchen garden book known to have been printed in America. In it were directions for growing "Salsify, or goat's beard, *Tragopogon*." Randolph surely knew that the second common name was a translation from the Greek—*trogos* for goat and *pogon*, beard—and was given to the plant on account of the silky supports of the purple rayed flowerheads. Today salsify is still grown in Williamsburg for its edible roots, and is regarded as a gourmet vegetable, whether purchased fresh or put up in cans or glass jars. Because the long, tapering, white skinned roots have a delicate oysterlike flavor, salsify is also known as oyster plant or vegetable oyster.

1 can (15 ounces) or jar (12½ ounces) salsify	¼ cup all-purpose flour
	1 cup hot milk
4 tablespoons butter	1 cup hot light cream
1 teaspoon onion, finely chopped	¼ teaspoon nutmeg
	dash of Tabasco sauce
6 sprigs of parsley, finely chopped	salt and white pepper to taste

Heat the salsify; drain.

Heat the butter, onion, and parsley together but do not brown.

Stir in the flour and continue stirring over low heat for 3 to 5 minutes.

Add the hot milk and cream and stir rapidly until the sauce is smooth.

Continue to stir until the sauce comes to a boil. Gently simmer, stirring, for 3 to 5 minutes longer.

Add the nutmeg and Tabasco sauce and season to taste.

Strain through a fine sieve.

Pour the cream sauce over the salsify and serve hot.

SALSIFY OR OYSTER PLANT FRITTERS
(4 servings)

1 can (15 ounces) or jar
  (12½ ounces) salsify
1 tablespoon parsley, chopped
Marinade:
  6 tablespoons salad oil
  3 tablespoons lemon juice

3 tablespoons all-purpose
  flour
⅓ cup lukewarm water
salt
1 teaspoon salad oil
1 egg white

Roll the pieces of salsify in the parsley and put them in a bowl.

Mix 6 tablespoons of the salad oil with the lemon juice, pour over the salsify, and marinate for 15 minutes. Drain well.

Combine the flour, water, a pinch of salt, and 1 teaspoon of salad oil and blend until smooth. Fold in the egg white, stiffly beaten.

Dip the pieces of salsify in the batter and fry in deep hot fat or oil (375° F.) for about 4 minutes or until they are golden brown.

Drain the fritters on paper towels, sprinkle with salt, and serve warm.

SCALLOPED TOMATOES
(4 servings)

1 small onion, chopped
4 tablespoons butter
1½ cups dry unseasoned
  bread cubes
½ cup light brown sugar

5 cups (2½ pounds)
  canned tomatoes
1 teaspoon salt
½ teaspoon pepper, freshly
  ground

Preheat the oven to 350° F.

Grease a shallow earthenware or other casserole.

Sauté the onion in butter until soft but not brown.

Add the bread cubes and brown sugar, stirring over low heat for 3 to 5 minutes.

Stir in the tomatoes; season to taste.

Put the tomatoes in the prepared casserole and bake at 350° F. for 30 to 40 minutes or until the casserole is bubbly.

CASCADES RATATOUILLE

(8–10 servings)

1½ pounds zucchini squash
3 ribs of celery
1 large onion
1 large green pepper
1 large eggplant
8 medium tomatoes
½ cup butter

3 cloves garlic, minced
1 tablespoon oregano
1 tablespoon basil
1 tablespoon salt
1 teaspoon pepper
4 tablespoons Parmesan
   cheese, grated

Preheat the oven to 350° F.

Grease a large shallow earthenware or other casserole.

Slice the zucchini and celery; cut the onion and green pepper into large squares; cut the eggplant into large cubes.

Scald the tomatoes in boiling water for 60 seconds, drain, remove the skin, and cut in half. Squeeze out and discard the tomato juice and seeds and cut each half into 4 pieces. Reserve.

Blanch the zucchini, celery, green pepper, and eggplant in boiling salted water until barely tender. Drain and reserve.

Sauté the onion in butter for 4 to 5 minutes.

Add the garlic, oregano, basil, salt, and pepper, and continue to sauté until the onion is transparent.

Combine all of the ingredients in the prepared casserole and sprinkle with the Parmesan cheese.

Bake at 350° F. for 20 to 25 minutes or until bubbly.

KING'S ARMS TAVERN
KIDNEY BEAN RELISH

(6 servings)

2 cans (15½ ounces each)
   kidney beans
1 medium red onion, thinly
   sliced
¼ cup white vinegar

¼ cup vegetable oil
½ teaspoon chives, snipped
½ teaspoon oregano
salt and freshly ground pepper
   to taste

Drain the beans. Add the onion.

Combine the white vinegar, vegetable oil, chives, and oregano and mix well.

Pour the dressing over the beans. Mix well.

Add salt and pepper to taste.

Refrigerate for 2 hours before serving.

KING'S ARMS TAVERN
CORN RELISH

(4 servings)

2 cups whole kernel corn
½ cup pickle relish
¼ cup red pepper relish

salt and freshly ground
pepper to taste

Drain all of the ingredients well.

Mix the ingredients together. Add salt and pepper to taste.

Chill before serving.

SCALLOPED TOMATOES
AND ARTICHOKE HEARTS

(6–8 servings)

1 can (2 pounds, 3 ounces)
whole plum tomatoes
1 can (14 ounces) artichoke
hearts
½ cup onion, finely chopped
2 tablespoons shallots, finely
chopped

¼ pound butter
½ teaspoon basil
2 tablespoons sugar
salt and pepper to taste

Preheat the oven to 325° F.

Grease a shallow earthenware or other casserole.

Drain the tomatoes and artichokes; rinse the artichokes in water and quarter them.

Sauté the onion and shallots in the butter until tender.

Add the tomatoes, artichokes, and basil; heat for 2 or 3 minutes, stirring gently. Season with the sugar, salt, and pepper.

Turn into the prepared casserole and bake at 325° F. for 10 to 15 minutes or until the vegetables are heated through.

Breads

The Bread in Gentlemen's Houses, is generally made of Wheat, but some rather choose the Pone, which is the Bread made of *Indian* Meal . . . and so called from the Indian name *Oppone*." So wrote Robert Beverley in 1705. No bread made from wheat was held to be nearly so sustaining as that made from corn; besides, the yield of corn per acre compared to that of wheat was better than twenty to one. But wheat flour was finer than cornmeal, and among the gentry buttered wheat bread and tea made a desirable snack between breakfast and early afternoon dinner. Corn bread was the bread to work and travel on. At Mount Vernon, "Indian cakes for breakfast after the Virginia fashion" was the rule.

Cornmeal could be made into more kinds of bread. The three mainstays—corn pone, ashcake, and hoecake—are similar to New England's journey or johnnycake, which is meal, water, and salt mixed into a stiff dough and shaped by hand. Pone was baked as the Indians baked it, in cakes before the fire. So was ashcake, "in Loaves on a warm Hearth, covering the Loaf with Leaves, then with warm Ashes, and afterwards with Coals over all." Ashcake was a staple of Negro cabins throughout the South before the Civil War. Hoecake was simply pone cooked on the blade of a hoe in the fireplace or over an open fire in the fields at noon by field workers.

The corn sticks and corn muffins featured on Williamsburg tavern menus are refinements of pone, being made from a medium batter and baked in molds in a hot oven.

INDIAN CORN MUFFINS

(1½ dozen)

1 cup white cornmeal
1 cup all-purpose flour
1 teaspoon salt
3 teaspoons baking powder

2 tablespoons sugar
2 eggs, lightly beaten
1 cup milk
3 tablespoons butter, melted

Preheat the oven to 400° F.

Grease muffin tins that are 1½ inches in diameter.

Sift the dry ingredients into a mixing bowl.

Combine the eggs, milk, and melted butter and add to the dry ingredients, mixing just until blended. Do not overmix.

Spoon into the greased muffin tins, filling each tin completely full. Bake at 400° F. for 20 minutes or until done.

CHRISTIANA CAMPBELL'S TAVERN SPOON BREAD

(8 servings)

Spoon bread, or batter bread, is a custardy corn bread served soufflé-hot from the dish, preferably earthenware, in which it is baked. It is said that the recipe "just happened" when a mixture used to make a corn bread enriched by milk and eggs was left forgotten in a hot oven. Virginians have ever since made spoon bread one of their favored foods. It is excellent served with herring roe, bacon, or fried apples.

1½ cups water
2 cups milk
1½ cups cornmeal
1¼ teaspoons salt

1½ teaspoons sugar
2 tablespoons butter
5 eggs
1 tablespoon baking powder

Preheat the oven to 350° F.

Grease a large shallow baking dish.

Combine the water and milk and heat to simmer.

Add the cornmeal, salt, sugar, and butter, and stir over medium heat until the mixture is thickened, about 5 minutes. Remove from the heat.

Beat the eggs with the baking powder until they are very light and fluffy, then add them to the cornmeal mixture. Mix well.

Pour into the prepared dish and bake at 350° F. for 45 to 50 minutes.

Serve hot.

GRITS SOUFFLÉ
(6 servings)

2 cups milk
½ cup instant grits
1 teaspoon salt
½ teaspoon baking powder

2 tablespoons butter, melted
½ teaspoon sugar
3 eggs, separated

Preheat the oven to 375° F.

Grease a 1½-quart casserole or 1½-quart soufflé dish.

Scald the milk, add the grits, and cook until thick, stirring constantly.

Add the salt, baking powder, butter, and sugar; mix well.

Beat the egg yolks and add to the grits.

Beat the egg whites until they hold soft peaks; fold in.

Pour into the prepared dish.

Bake at 375° F. for 30 minutes.

Serve hot.

Note: Just before folding in the egg whites, ½ cup grated sharp cheese and a dash of Tabasco sauce can be added to make an excellent variation of the above recipe.

CHRISTIANA CAMPBELL'S TAVERN
SWEET POTATO MUFFINS
(3 dozen)

1 medium sweet potato
¼ cup butter
½ cup sugar
1 egg, lightly beaten
¼ teaspoon lemon peel,
    grated
1 cup all-purpose flour
2 teaspoons baking powder

½ teaspoon baking soda
½ teaspoon salt
½ teaspoon cinnamon
¼ teaspoon nutmeg
½ cup milk
¼ cup walnuts, chopped
¼ cup golden raisins,
    chopped

Preheat the oven to 375° F.

Scrub the sweet potato and prick it in several places with a fork.

Bake the sweet potato at 375° F. for 45 minutes or until tender. Cool to room temperature.

Peel the sweet potato. Mash the sweet potato with a fork and reserve ⅔ cup.

Preheat the oven to 400° F.

Grease mini-muffin tins that are 1⅞ inches in diameter × ⅞ inch deep.

Cream the butter and sugar. Beat in the reserved ⅔ cup of sweet potato. Beat in the egg and grated lemon peel.

Sift the flour with the baking powder, baking soda, salt, cinnamon, and nutmeg.

Add the dry ingredients and milk alternately by hand, mixing just until blended. Do not overmix.

Fold in the chopped nuts and raisins.

Spoon into the greased muffin tins, filling each tin ¾ full. A little sugar and cinnamon may be sprinkled on top of each muffin if desired.

Bake at 400° F. for 20 minutes.

SALLY LUNN

According to tradition, Sally Lunn is named after a young girl who in the eighteenth century "cried" the sweet yeast bread that bears her name in the streets of England's fashionable spa, Bath. Some now doubt whether Sally Lunn really existed and suggest other sources for the name. Who knows? But Sally Lunn does have a place in the *Oxford English Dictionary*, and hers was a household name in the southern colonies as it was in England.

1 cup milk	*⅓ cup sugar*
½ cup shortening	*2 teaspoons salt*
4 cups sifted all-purpose flour, divided	*2 packages active dry yeast*
	3 eggs

Preheat the oven to 350° F. 10 minutes before the Sally Lunn is ready to be baked.

Grease a 10-inch tube cake pan or a bundt pan.

Heat the milk, shortening, and ¼ cup of water until very warm—about 120° F. The shortening does not need to melt.

Blend 1⅓ cups of flour with the sugar, salt, and dry yeast in a large mixing bowl.

Blend the warm liquids into the flour mixture. Beat with an electric mixer at medium speed for about 2 minutes, scraping the sides of the bowl occasionally.

Gradually add ⅔ cup of the remaining flour and the eggs and beat at high speed for 2 minutes.

Add the remaining flour and mix well. The batter will be thick but not stiff.

Cover and let the dough rise in a warm, draft-free place (about 85° F.) until it doubles in bulk—about 1 hour and 15 minutes.

Beat the dough down with a spatula or at the lowest speed on an electric mixer and turn into the prepared pan.

Cover and let rise in a warm, draft-free place until it has increased in bulk ⅓ to ½—about 30 minutes.

Bake for 40 to 50 minutes at 350° F.

Run a knife around the center and outer edges of the bread and turn it onto a plate to cool.

MRS. BOOTH'S BISCUIT MIX
(4½ cups)

3 cups self-rising flour
1½ teaspoons baking powder
1 tablespoon sugar

1 cup shortening
milk
melted butter or milk

Preheat the oven to 450° F. 10 minutes before the biscuits are to go in.

Grease a cookie sheet.

Sift the dry ingredients into a mixing bowl.

Cut in the shortening with knives or a pastry blender until it is evenly distributed.

Store in a covered container in the refrigerator.

For 6 biscuits, 2 inches in diameter, combine 1 cup of mix with enough milk to moisten.

Knead lightly on a floured surface 5 or 6 times.

Roll out the dough ½ inch thick for high biscuits; ¼ inch thick for thin crusty biscuits. Cut with a biscuit cutter.

Place on the prepared cookie sheet and brush the tops with melted butter or milk. Space the dough close together for soft biscuits; 1 inch apart for crusty ones.

Bake at 450° F. for 8 to 10 minutes or until golden brown.

PECAN WAFFLES
(6–8 servings)

Holy bread in twelfth-century England were small especially stamped wafers made from fine-textured flour. Ordinary wafers, or waffles, were larger, thicker, and more substantial. Chaucer mentions them in the *Canterbury Tales*, and many a poet who bought his wafer piping hot on the street or at a stall beside the church door sang its praises. Homemade wafers had a sweetened sauce poured over them. They were baked in irons, either round or square, which were long-handled for holding over the coals of an open fire.

For more than 250 years after King Henry VIII's break with Rome, wafers were forgotten in Great Britain—until some Dutch migrants to Paisley, Scotland, introduced their *wafelijzer*, which an English cookbook called "The Right Dutch Wafer," and which we in America now call the waffle.

Thomas Jefferson first tasted waffles in Holland in 1789 and there bought a pair of waffle irons with tongs for one and one-third Dutch florins.

2⅔ cups sifted all-purpose flour
3 tablespoons sugar
4 teaspoons baking powder
1 teaspoon salt
4 eggs, separated

2⅔ cups milk
½ cup plus 1 tablespoon butter, melted
⅓ cup chopped pecans

Sift the dry ingredients together.
Beat the egg yolks until thick.
Combine the beaten yolks with the milk and melted butter and stir into the dry ingredients.
Add the pecans, mixing only until blended.

Beat the egg whites until stiff and fold them into the batter. Bake in a hot waffle iron.

(4–5 servings)

1½ cups sifted all-purpose flour
1½ tablespoons sugar
2½ teaspoons baking powder
½ teaspoon salt

3 eggs, separated
1½ cups milk
5 tablespoons butter, melted
¼ cup chopped pecans

Follow the instructions above.

MANCHET BREAD

Wheat flour has always been acknowledged as the best for making white bread. England's bakers, from the fourteenth century onward, called bread made from fine quality wheat flour manchet bread.

Today many people, especially young people, are showing an increased interest in foods that contain no preservatives. Chiefly for this reason, Colonial Williamsburg has added a quality bread made from a fine unbleached wheat flour, stone-ground as it used to be in colonial times, to its menus, and has revived the name manchet for it.

3½ to 4 cups sifted unbleached
    natural flour, divided
1 package active
    dry yeast
2 tablespoons sugar

1½ teaspoons salt
1 cup warm water
¼ cup butter
1 egg, at room temperature

Combine 1 cup of flour with the dry yeast, sugar, and salt in the large bowl of an electric mixer; mix thoroughly.

Heat the water with the butter over low heat until very warm (120° to 130° F.).

Gradually add the liquids to the dry ingredients. Beat at medium speed for 2 minutes, scraping the bowl occasionally.

Add ½ cup of flour, or enough flour to make a thick batter. Add the egg and beat at high speed for 2 minutes. Keep scraping the bowl.

Stir in enough additional flour to make a soft dough—approximately 1½ cups.

Turn the dough onto a lightly floured board and knead until it is smooth and elastic, about 8 to 10 minutes, using the remaining flour as needed. *The kneading time is important.*

Place the dough in a greased bowl, turning to grease the top. Cover with a moist cloth and let it rise in a warm, draft-free place (about 85° F.) until double in bulk—about 1 to 1½ hours. Keep the covering cloth moist.

Grease a 9¼ x 5¼ x 2¾-inch loaf pan.

Punch the dough down and turn it out onto a lightly floured board. Cover; let it rest 15 minutes. Roll it into a uniform thickness in a 9 x 12-inch rectangle. Beginning with the upper 9-inch side, roll toward you, jelly roll style. Seal with thumbs or heel of hand. Seal the ends; fold the sealed ends under. Be careful not to tear the dough. Place in the prepared pan.

Cover with the moist cloth and let it rise in a warm, draft-free place until double in bulk, about 1 hour.

When the dough is near the end of the rising time, preheat the oven to 350° F.

Place the loaf in the oven on the center shelf and bake at 350° F. for 40 minutes, or until done.

Remove from the pan immediately and cool on a rack.

WILLIAMSBURG INN YORKSHIRE PUDDING

(*6–8 servings*)

There are probably as many ways to make Yorkshire Pudding as there are to make bread. The word "pudding" implies a somewhat solid dish, but Yorkshire Pudding should be light, puffy, crisp, and brown. It should be ready to serve at the same moment as the beef, for which it is the superb accompaniment. Colonial Williamsburg adds a refinement of former days that most housewives cannot manage today—the meat drips onto the pudding as it finishes cooking.

2 *eggs*
1 *cup milk*
1 *cup all-purpose flour*
salt and pepper to taste

pinch nutmeg
½ *cup melted fat* or *beef*
    drippings, divided

Preheat oven to 425° F. 10 minutes before pudding is ready to go in.

Beat eggs for 1 minute with an electric mixer on highest speed.

Add milk and gradually beat in the flour.

Add seasoning and 2 tablespoons of melted fat or drippings and beat 1 minute on highest speed. Let stand at room temperature at least 30 minutes.

Place remaining fat in a 7½-inch black skillet to cover the bottom by ⅛ inch and heat in the oven until sizzling hot.

Add mixture and bake at 425° F. for 30 minutes.

Reduce heat to 350° F. and bake an additional 10 to 15 minutes.

Do not be dismayed when center falls—this is characteristic of Yorkshire Pudding.

Note: It would be helpful to save drippings from previous roasts to use in making this dish.

WILLIAMSBURG INN POPOVERS

(*8–10 servings*)

Liberally grease 8 or 10 custard cups.

Follow recipe for Yorkshire Pudding (*page 114*) but omit the pepper. Butter can be substituted for drippings.

Pour batter into prepared, heated custard cups, filling not more than ⅓ full.

Bake at 425° F. for 30 minutes, then turn off oven. Allow popovers to remain in oven 5 to 10 minutes longer.

Serve immediately.

Desserts

Wrote an eighteenth-century poet:

> 'Tis the Desert that graces all the Feast,
> For an ill end disparages the rest. . . .

The dessert was the pride and joy of colonial Virginia's housewives. A "Collation of Sweetmeats" was customarily served at plantation house balls or on great occasions at the Governor's Palace, or sometimes in the Capitol. William Byrd II set down in his diary:

> About 7 o'clock the company went in coaches from the Governor's house to the capitol where the Governor opened the ball with a French dance with my wife. . . . Then we danced country dances for an hour and the company was carried into another room where was a very fine collation of sweetmeats.

On one occasion the long tables bore one hundred dishes of creams and jellies, confectionery of all sorts, candied fruits, and sugared nuts.

In the *Virginia Gazette* of October 6, 1738, Mrs. Stagg of Williamsburg gave notice that she had for sale hartshorn and calves-feet jellies, fresh every Tuesday and Friday:

> Also Curran Jellies, & many other sorts of Fruit Jellies: Mackaroons, and Savoy Biscakes; and all sorts of Confectionary, in small Quantities, or large if wanted, every Day, at very reasonable Rates. She has a considerable Quantity of choice Barbadoes Sweet-meats, which are to be sold in small Pots, or a smaller Quantity.

Those were the days of the flummery and the floating island, the first being made of milk, flour, and eggs, and the other of little cakes topped with egg white and set afloat on a sea of syllabub. The syllabub

118

itself was a standard drink or dish, rich or simple, fundamentally of milk or cream with wine, sugar, and other flavorings, sometimes curdled and sometimes "whipt." The simplest variety was Syllabub-under-the-Cow, made in a quick trip to the cow barn to draw a fine warm froth of milk directly into a bowl of wine. Its name was derived from "Sill," the name of its French wine, and from "bub," the Elizabethan nickname for a bubbling drink.

Gone now are the flummeries, the floating islands, the syllabubs. No longer are there enough hands, nor is there enough time, for the making of elaborate creams and cakes except by professionals. Too, tastes have changed. We have become content to sample one dessert at a time—ice cream or sherbet, pudding, cream or mousse, or pie— and to watch our weight.

CHRISTIANA CAMPBELL'S TAVERN
TIPSY SQUIRE
(*10 servings*)

This is the American version of the nineteenth-century English tipsy cake. Although Tipsy Squire is fully capable of justifying its name, gourmets will not overlook the squire's noble counterpart, the English Trifle.

The Trifle is no trifling matter. Many versions exist, yet for the true trifle—one of the most exotic of desserts—there is no simplified substitute.

Colonial Williamsburg uses fresh fruit as well as jam in its ingredients, but in every other particular uses the prescribed ingredients for the classic dish. The purists' rules are also followed: that only sherry—no other wine—be used for flavoring, and that the trifle be made in a crystal dish.

119

½ cup shortening
1 cup sugar
2 eggs
2¼ cups sifted all-purpose flour
3 teaspoons baking powder
½ teaspoon salt

¾ cup milk
1 teaspoon vanilla
SHERRY CUSTARD (*below*)
whipped cream
toasted slivered almonds

Preheat the oven to 350° F.

Grease and lightly flour a 9 x 9 x 2-inch or 7½ x 11½ x 2-inch baking pan.

Cream the shortening and sugar.

Add the eggs and beat until the mixture is lemon colored and fluffy.

Add the sifted dry ingredients alternately with the milk, beating well after each addition.

Add the vanilla with the last addition of milk.

Pour into the prepared cake pan.

Bake at 350° F. for 35 to 40 minutes or until the cake tests done.

Cool on a cake rack before cutting into portions.

To serve, place a portion of cake in a dessert bowl and pour the Sherry Custard over it.

Garnish with the sweetened whipped cream and toasted almonds.

SHERRY CUSTARD

1 quart milk
¾ cup sugar
3 tablespoons cornstarch
⅛ teaspoon salt

3 egg yolks
1 egg
1 teaspoon rum flavoring
½ cup cream sherry

Cook the milk, sugar, cornstarch, and salt in a heavy saucepan over medium heat, stirring constantly, until slightly thickened.

Beat the egg yolks and 1 whole egg.

Add 1 cup of the hot milk mixture to the beaten egg yolks, stir, and return to the hot milk.

Continue cooking, stirring constantly, but do not boil, until of custard consistency.

Add the rum flavoring and sherry.

Cool and serve over the cake.

Note: Sometimes, in spite of every precaution, the custard separates. When this happens, remove the custard from the heat immediately and place it in a bowl of cracked ice. Beat rapidly until smoothness is restored. The custard will be slightly thinner.

CHERRY TRIFLE
(8–10 servings)

2 cups Vanilla Cream Custard (page 141), divided
2 dozen ladyfingers or 1 layer of spongecake cut into fingers, divided
1 cup cherry jam, divided
rind of 1 lemon, grated and divided
½ cup dry sherry, divided

3 tablespoons brandy, divided
1 quart fresh cherries or 1 can (1 pound, 5 ounces) cherry pie filling, divided
1 dozen macaroons, crushed and divided
1 cup whipping cream
maraschino cherries

Prepare the Custard Sauce.

Coat ½ of the ladyfingers with ½ cup of cherry jam; place in the bottom of a crystal bowl 8 inches in diameter and 3½ inches deep, and sprinkle with ½ of the lemon rind.

Sprinkle with ¼ cup of sherry and ½ of the brandy.

Cover with a layer of ½ of the cherries or cherry pie filling and ½ of the macaroons. Allow to stand an hour or so.

Pour ½ of the Custard Sauce over the top, repeat the layers of ladyfingers, cherry jam, lemon rind, sherry, brandy, cherries, and the remaining macaroons. Repeat the custard layer. Chill.

Just before serving, top with whipped cream and maraschino cherries.

AMBROSIA
(6 servings)

3 fresh oranges
3 fresh grapefruit
½ small fresh pineapple
⅓ cup orange juice

¼ cup light corn syrup
½ cup flaked or fresh coconut, shredded

Peel and section the oranges and grapefruit.

Peel and dice the pineapple and mix it with the orange and grapefruit sections.

Combine the orange juice and syrup.

Divide the fruit mixture into 6 sherbet glasses, pour the juice over the fruit, and top with the coconut.

Note: Whole blueberries or sliced strawberries can be added to the above for color as well as flavor.

Also note: A little dry sherry can be mixed with the orange juice for a different flavor. If sherry is added, allow the mixture to ripen overnight.

FRESH STRAWBERRY MOUSSE
(*8–10 servings*)

This is certainly a dish to set before a queen, as indeed it was at the dinner given in honor of Queen Elizabeth II and Prince Philip at the Williamsburg Inn. And there was something especially appropriate in the choice of this dessert.

When the first Virginia settlers stepped ashore in the spring of 1607, they found strawberries in a little plot of ground in a clearing of the forest. They were reminded instantly of home, only the berries were "foure times bigger and better" than those in England. One enthusiast claimed that they were so thick on the ground that men's shoes were stained red with their juice as they walked among them.

1 pint strawberries
2 packages (3 ounces each) strawberry flavor gelatin

¼ cup sugar
1 pint whipping cream

Crush the strawberries and drain the juice; reserve. Add enough water to the juice to make 1½ cups.

Bring the juice to a boil and stir in the gelatin; dissolve and cool.

Add the strawberries and sugar.

Whip the cream until it stands in soft peaks and fold it into the strawberry mixture.

Pour the mixture into a 2-quart ring mold or a 1½-quart soufflé dish with a 2-inch collar.

Chill several hours or overnight.

Note: Two packages (10 ounces each) of frozen strawberries can be substituted for the fresh strawberries. Omit the sugar if frozen berries are used.

KING'S ARMS TAVERN OLD-FASHIONED RAISIN RICE PUDDING

(8 servings)

4 eggs
¾ cup sugar
2 cups milk
1⅓ cups cooked rice
1½ teaspoons lemon juice

1½ teaspoons vanilla
1 tablespoon butter, melted
1 teaspoon nutmeg
⅔ cup seedless raisins

Preheat the oven to 350° F.

Grease a 2-quart casserole.

Combine the eggs, sugar, and milk and beat well.

Fold in the rice, lemon juice, vanilla, melted butter, nutmeg, and raisins.

Pour into the prepared casserole and put the dish in a pan of boiling water.

Bake at 350° F. for approximately 45 minutes or until the custard is set.

WINE JELLY MOLD WITH CUSTARD SAUCE

(10–12 servings)

4 envelopes unflavored gelatin
2 cups sugar
6 tablespoons lemon juice
rind of 3 lemons, grated

2½ cups burgundy
CUSTARD SAUCE *(page 124)* or
   whipped cream and red
   glazed cherries

Soften the gelatin in 1½ cups of cold water for 5 minutes.

Dissolve the sugar in 1 quart of hot water and bring to a boil, then remove from the heat.

Add the lemon juice, rind, and softened gelatin, allow to set 5 minutes, then strain the mixture through a cheesecloth.

Add the burgundy, stirring gently to avoid making air bubbles.

Pour slowly into an 8-cup mold and chill several hours or until firm.

Unmold onto a chilled serving dish.

Serve with Custard Sauce or garnish lightly with whipped cream and red glazed cherries.

CUSTARD SAUCE

1½ tablespoons cornstarch   *½ cup sugar*
2 cups light cream, divided   *1 teaspoon vanilla*
4 egg yolks

Dissolve the cornstarch in ¼ cup of cream.

Beat the egg yolks until light, then combine with the cornstarch.

Heat the remaining cream, taking care not to boil, and add the sugar.

Pour 1 cup of hot cream and sugar over the egg mixture, stirring constantly.

Return the cream to low heat, stir in the egg-cream mixture, and continue to stir and cook 5 minutes until the sauce is slightly thickened.

Add the vanilla, blend thoroughly, and cool.

WILLIAMSBURG LODGE
BAVARIAN CREAM
(4–5 servings)

1 envelope unflavored gelatin   *1 cup milk*
4 egg yolks   *1 cup whipping cream*
dash of salt   *2 teaspoons vanilla*
½ cup sugar

Soften the gelatin in ¼ cup of cold water; set aside.

Mix the egg yolks, salt, and sugar together in the top of a double boiler.

Gradually blend in the milk and cook over hot water, stirring constantly, until thick and smooth.

Add the softened gelatin, stirring until dissolved. Cool.

Whip the cream, add the vanilla, and fold in gently.

Spoon into a 1-quart mold or 4 or 5 sherbet or parfait glasses. Chill.

Note: For a lighter Bavarian Cream, beat the egg whites and add before the whipped cream. This will make 8 servings.

CHOCOLATE BAVARIAN CREAM

Follow the instructions for Williamsburg Lodge Bavarian Cream (page 124).

Decrease the vanilla to 1 teaspoon.

Before cooling the egg-gelatin mixture, add 2 ounces of unsweetened chocolate, melted.

LIQUEUR BAVARIAN CREAM

Follow the instructions for Williamsburg Lodge Bavarian Cream (page 124).

Omit the vanilla.

Add 2 tablespoons of any flavor liqueur to the whipped cream.

SHIELDS TAVERN
SYLLABUBS
(6–8 servings)

1½ cups whipping cream   *½ cup white wine*
rind and juice of 2 lemons   *¼ cup dry sherry*
½ cup sugar   *whipped cream (optional)*

Whisk the whipping cream by hand until it thickens a bit.

Add the lemon rind, lemon juice, sugar, white wine, and sherry one at a time, whisking by hand after each addition.

Whisk the mixture for 3 to 5 minutes until thickened. Keep in mind that too much whipping will turn it to butter.

Pour immediately into parfait glasses and refrigerate overnight. The mixture will separate when it stands.

If desired, pile whipped cream on top of each glass before serving.

Note: Allowing the filled parfait glasses to stand for 1 to 2 hours before refrigerating will result in even greater separation of the mixture.

WILLIAMSBURG LODGE
MOCHA VELVET CREAM
(6–8 servings)

1 envelope unflavored gelatin	*2½ tablespoons instant coffee*
1½ cups milk, divided	*4 eggs, separated*
¾ cup sugar, divided	*1 teaspoon vanilla*
½ teaspoon salt	*1 cup whipping cream*

Sprinkle the gelatin over ¼ cup of milk; set aside to soften.

Combine ½ cup of sugar with the salt, coffee, and egg yolks in the top of a double boiler.

Gradually add the remaining milk. Cook over hot water, stirring constantly, until thickened and smooth.

Add the softened gelatin and cook, stirring constantly, until dissolved.

Remove from the heat, add the vanilla, and chill until slightly thickened.

Reserve 1 tablespoon of the remaining sugar for the whipping cream, and beat the egg whites with the rest of the sugar until they are stiff but not dry. Fold into the gelatin mixture.

Whip the cream and gently fold half of it into the gelatin-egg white mixture.

Spoon into 6 to 8 individual dessert dishes and chill until set.

Top with the remaining whipped cream sweetened with the reserved sugar.

Ice Creams and Sherbets

Sherbets were the forerunners of ice cream. The Chinese taught the Hindus, the Persians, and the Arabs the art of making water ices, or sherbets. A Sicilian who got around introduced them into France about 1660 and later opened a café specializing in sherbets in Paris. Sherbets became the rage, and in due course ice creams followed. Soon there were around 250 shops and restaurants in Paris that were officially licensed to make and sell ice creams and water ices.

Wealthy Marylanders appear to have learned about ice cream before Virginians did. Governor Thomas Bladen's French wife may have introduced them there. On May 19, 1744, William Black, a Virginian on official business in Annapolis, attended a dinner at the governor's mansion and later reported:

> We were Received by his Excellency and his Lady in the Hall, where we were an hour Entertain'd by the Governor, with some Glasses of Punch in the intervals of the Discourse; then the Scene was chang'd to a Dining Room, where you saw a Table in the most Splendent manner set out with a Great Variety of Dishes, all serv'd up in the most Elegant way, after which came a Dessert no less Curious; Among the Rarities of which it was Compos'd, was some fine Ice Cream which, with the Strawberries and Milk, eat most Deliciously.

Governor Francis Fauquier of Virginia wrote his brother that in July 1758 a hailstorm provided a supply of ice, which he used to cool wine and to freeze cream.

In May 1784, George Washington recorded in his diary that he had spent one pound, thirteen shillings, and fourpence on a "cream machine for ice."

In a letter dated August 16, 1799, Mrs. Anne Blair Banister wrote from Shannon Hill to her niece: "Yesterday we were at Mr. Baylors, & made myself sick with Ice-Creams, Water Melons, Plumbs &c—(so has Mr. Cary. . . . Alas! so much frigidity does not suit us old folks)."

VANILLA ICE CREAM
(*1 gallon*)

2 tablespoons cornstarch
2 quarts milk, divided
4 eggs, separated
2 cups sugar

½ teaspoon salt
2 teaspoons vanilla
1 pint whipping cream

Dissolve the cornstarch in 1 cup of milk.

Heat the remaining milk and add the cornstarch, stirring constantly.

Add the well-beaten egg yolks and sugar.

Stir constantly and cook over low heat until the mixture coats a metal spoon.

Cool several hours or overnight in the refrigerator, if possible.

When ready to freeze, beat the egg whites, salt, and vanilla to a froth and add to the chilled milk mixture.

Stir in the cream and pour the mixture into a 5-quart freezer container. Follow the manufacturer's directions for freezing.

CHRISTIANA CAMPBELL'S TAVERN
FIG ICE CREAM
(*3 quarts*)

4 eggs, separated
1¼ cups sugar, divided
2 cups milk, scalded
3 tablespoons lemon juice

1 pint light cream
½ cup cream sherry
1 teaspoon vanilla
1 quart figs, crushed or *puréed*

Beat the egg yolks and ½ cup plus 2 tablespoons of sugar.

Add the milk slowly, stirring constantly.

Cook over low heat until quite hot, but do not boil.

Combine the egg whites with the remaining sugar and beat to a light froth.

Pour the cooked egg-milk mixture into the egg whites, stirring constantly.

Stir in the lemon juice.

Add the cream, sherry, vanilla, and figs, blending well.

Pour the mixture into a 5-quart freezer container. Follow the manufacturer's directions for freezing.

KING'S ARMS TAVERN
GREENGAGE PLUM ICE CREAM

(3 quarts)

Greengage Plum Ice Cream was a happy accident. One of Williamsburg's taverns happened to be out of the usual flavorings for ice cream that day. The greengage plum came to the rescue, and now flavors one of the most popular ice creams at the King's Arms, where it has become a specialty.

"All plums," said the herbalist Nicholas Culpeper, "are under Venus, and are like women—some better and some worse." The greengage plum is the accepted queen of plums; a wilding of the Caucasus, it wandered through Italy and France to become known there as Reine Claude, after the wife of François I. Reine Claude kept wandering, and in America left an offspring known as the Jefferson greengage.

5 eggs, separated
1½ cups sugar, divided
2 cups milk
3 cups fresh or canned (1
  pound, 12 ounces)
  greengage plums, drained
  and stoned

1½ pints light cream
⅓ cup lemon juice
green food coloring

Beat the egg yolks together with 1 cup of sugar.

Heat the milk almost to boiling and pour 1 cup over the beaten egg yolks, stirring until well blended.

Return the egg-milk mixture to the hot milk and cook, but do not boil, over medium heat, stirring constantly, until the mixture coats a metal spoon; cool.

Beat the egg whites with ½ cup of sugar and, when the egg mixture is cool, combine the two, mixing well.

Purée the plums in a food processor or a blender.

Add the plums, cream, and lemon juice gradually to the egg mixture.

Add the green food coloring, a few drops at a time, until the desired pistachio green tint is achieved.

Pour the mixture into a 5-quart freezer container. Follow the manufacturer's directions for freezing.

Note: Ice cream should be allowed to "ripen" at least four hours after freezing to bring out the delicate greengage plum flavor.

Also note: If fresh greengage plums are used, they should be blanched 60 seconds in hot water before the skins are removed.

CHOWNING'S TAVERN
BLACK WALNUT ICE CREAM

(1½ quarts)

Farmers of the eastern seaboard states, where the black walnut is native, spent many a winter evening before the open fire cracking and eating walnuts. A nut of such fine taste just had to find its way into ice cream.

8 egg yolks	*2 cups whipping cream*
1¼ cups sugar	*1 teaspoon black walnut*
dash of salt	*flavoring*
2 cups milk	*1 cup black walnuts, chopped*

Beat the egg yolks with the sugar until creamy; add the salt.

Bring the milk and cream almost to boiling; remove from the heat and pour slowly into the egg mixture, stirring constantly.

Return to low heat, stirring constantly to avoid scorching, but do not boil. Add the black walnut flavoring. Heat to scalding.

Pour the mixture into a 1-gallon freezer container. Follow the manufacturer's directions for freezing.

When the dasher is removed, add the black walnuts, stirring to distribute them evenly.

Pack as freezing instructions direct and allow to "ripen" at least 3 hours before serving.

ORANGE SHERBET

(*2 quarts*)

1½ *cups sugar*
1 *cup light corn syrup*
1 *can* (*12 ounces*) *frozen*
   orange juice concentrate

1 *can* (*6 ounces*) *frozen*
   lemonade concentrate
rind of 1 orange, grated

Boil the sugar in 6 cups of water for 5 minutes.

Add the corn syrup, juices, and rind.

Cool and strain. Pour the mixture into a 1-gallon freezer container. Follow the manufacturer's directions for freezing.

RASPBERRY ICE

(*3 quarts*)

4 *packages* (*10 ounces each*)
   frozen red raspberries
1 *can* (*6 ounces*) *frozen*
   lemonade concentrate

2¼ *cups sugar, divided*
1 *envelope unflavored gelatin*
2 *egg whites*

Thaw the raspberries, purée them in a food processor or in a blender, press them through a sieve to remove the seeds, and combine with the thawed lemonade concentrate.

Mix 4 cups of water and 2 cups of sugar and boil over medium heat for 5 minutes. Cool.

Soften the gelatin in ¼ cup of water. Stir the softened gelatin into the cooling sugar syrup; continue stirring until the gelatin is dissolved.

Combine the sugar and raspberry mixtures.

Beat the egg whites with the remaining sugar and add to the raspberry mixture. Blend well.

Pour the mixture into a 1-gallon freezer container. Follow the manufacturer's directions for freezing.

Pastries

Some liked bread made of wheat flour and others preferred it of corn-meal, but there was one reason why early Virginia housewives had to have wheat flour on hand. Cornmeal is no good for pastry making; the dough does not "spread." After all, early Virginians were almost all of English stock, and what Englishman would be without his pie—a dish of meat, fowl, fish, fruit, or vegetables enclosed or covered with a layer of paste and baked.

Properly a pie, like the English garden, is enclosed. A tart is open and smaller, brought into England no doubt from the Continent. The American pie, as we know it, is a compromise between the pie and the tart: it is not baked as it so often was in England—or in Mrs. Campbell's tavern—in a deep pie dish, but when it contains the Old World fruits of apple, cherry, peach, or apricot, it is enclosed with crust in a pie pan. Pies made of New World pumpkin and pecan are open like tarts.

PASTRY CRUST MIX

(4 cups)

3 cups all-purpose flour   1 cup shortening
1 teaspoon salt   ice water
2 teaspoons sugar

Mix the dry ingredients together.

Blend in the shortening with knives or a pastry blender until the mixture is of pebbly consistency.

Store in a covered container in the refrigerator.

When needed, measure out these amounts:

	Single Crust	Double Crust
8-inch pie	1 to 1¼ cups	2 to 2¼ cups
9-inch pie	1½ cups	2½ cups
10-inch pie	1¾ cups	2¾ cups
12 tart shells	2¾ cups	

Moisten the pastry mix with enough ice water to hold the dough together when pushed lightly with a fork.

Roll out on a lightly floured board or pastry cloth.

Note: When a recipe calls for prebaked shell or shells, line the pan with dough, prick well with a fork, and bake at 425° F. for 12 to 15 minutes or until golden brown.

(8 cups)

6 cups all-purpose flour   2 cups shortening
2 teaspoons salt   ice water
4 teaspoons sugar

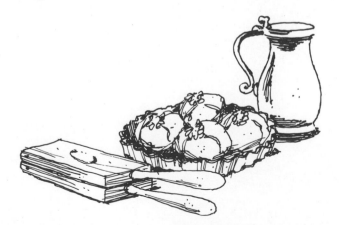

APPLE PIE

(one 9-inch pie)

Apple pie is the beginning of the kitchen alphabet for English-speaking children the world over, and for many a man, as for many a boy, it is the pie of pies. A distinct line is drawn by good cooks between a cooking and an eating apple, or, as purists say, between a culinary and a dessert apple. Old varieties are hard to come by. Rome Beauty is Colonial Williamsburg's favorite culinary apple.

PASTRY CRUST MIX *for 9-inch double crust pie (page 133)*
1¼ to 1½ *cups sugar*
⅛ *teaspoon salt*
¾ *teaspoon cinnamon*
½ *teaspoon nutmeg*

2 *tablespoons all-purpose flour*
6 to 8 *tart apples (2 to 2½ pounds), peeled and sliced*
lemon juice (optional)
½ *teaspoon lemon rind, grated*
1 to 2 *tablespoons butter*

Preheat the oven to 425° F.

Roll the pastry for the bottom crust over a rolling pin for ease in lining the pan. Cover the pastry for the top crust while filling the pie to keep it moist.

Mix the dry ingredients together in a large bowl.

Add the sliced apples and mix to coat.

Place the apple slices in the pan, laying slices first along the outside and then working toward the center until the bottom of the pastry is covered.

Continue placing slices in the same way until the pan is filled. Sprinkle with the lemon juice and rind and dot with the butter. Moisten the edge of the bottom crust.

Roll the top crust around a rolling pin, unroll over the apple filling, and trim to ½ inch larger than the pie pan. Press the edges firmly together, flute, and slash vents in the center of the crust.

Bake at 425° F. for 15 minutes, then reduce the heat to 350° F. and bake for 40 to 45 minutes or until the apples are done and the crust is golden brown.

APPLE DUMPLINGS

(6 dumplings)

PASTRY CRUST MIX *for 10-inch double crust pie (page 133)*
6 *whole large apples, peeled and cored*

1½ *cups sugar, divided*
¾ *teaspoon cinnamon, divided*
¼ *teaspoon nutmeg*
6 *tablespoons butter, divided*

Preheat the oven to 450° F. 10 minutes before the dumplings are ready to be baked.

Roll out the pastry ⅛ inch thick and cut it into six 7-inch squares.

Place an apple in the center of each square.

Fill the apples with a mixture of ½ cup of sugar, ½ teaspoon of cinnamon, ¼ teaspoon of nutmeg, and 2 tablespoons of butter.

Moisten the edges of the pastry with cold water and fold them up around the apples, pressing the edges together to seal firmly. Prick the pastry in several places.

Chill 1 hour.

Combine the remaining sugar, cinnamon, butter, and 2 cups of hot water and boil 5 minutes.

Place the apples in a 9 x 12-inch baking dish and bake at 450° F. for 10 minutes.

Reduce the heat to 350° F., pour the syrup over the apples, and bake 35 minutes, basting occasionally.

CHRISTIANA CAMPBELL'S TAVERN RUM CREAM PIE

(one 9-inch pie)

CRUMB CRUST *(page 136)*
1 *envelope unflavored gelatin*
5 *egg yolks*
1 *cup sugar*

⅓ *cup dark rum*
1½ *cups whipping cream*
unsweetened chocolate

Prepare a Crumb Crust (*below*).

Soften the gelatin in ½ cup of cold water. Place over low heat and bring almost to a boil, stirring to dissolve.

Beat the egg yolks and sugar until very light.

Stir the gelatin into the egg mixture; cool.

Gradually add the rum, beating constantly.

Whip the cream until it stands in soft peaks and fold it into the gelatin mixture.

Cool until the mixture begins to set, then spoon it into the Crumb Crust and chill until firm enough to cut.

Grate the unsweetened chocolate over the top before serving.

CRUMB CRUST

2¼ cups graham cracker
  crumbs
½ cup butter, melted

2 tablespoons sugar
½ teaspoon cinnamon

Combine the ingredients and press into a 9-inch pie pan. Chill.

EGGNOG PIE

(one 9-inch pie)

PASTRY CRUST MIX *for 9-inch
  pie shell (page 133),* or CRUMB
  CRUST *(above)*
1 envelope unflavored gelatin
1 cup milk

¾ cup sugar, divided
3 eggs, separated
¼ cup light or dark rum
1 cup whipping cream
nutmeg

Prepare and bake the pie shell, or chill the Crumb Crust.

Soften the gelatin in ¼ cup of water; set aside.

Bring the milk and ½ cup of sugar to a boil.

Beat the egg yolks.

Add ½ cup of hot milk and the sugar mixture to the eggs, stir, and return the egg mixture to the remaining hot milk and sugar mixture.

Cook, stirring, but not boiling, until the custard coats a metal spoon.

Stir in the gelatin and rum.

Cool in the refrigerator until the mixture begins to set.

Beat the egg whites with 3 tablespoons of sugar until soft peaks form. Fold into the custard.

Whip the cream and fold in 1 cup.

Spoon into the pie shell.

Beat 1 tablespoon of sugar into the remaining whipped cream and spread on the pie.

Sprinkle with nutmeg and chill until ready to serve.

Note: This pie freezes well. It needs to be removed from the freezer only a few minutes before serving.

SWEET POTATO PIE

(one 9-inch pie)

PASTRY CRUST MIX *for 9-inch pie shell (page 133)*
1½ cups canned sweet potatoes, mashed
⅔ cup granulated sugar
2 tablespoons butter, melted
½ teaspoon nutmeg

½ teaspoon mace
½ teaspoon vanilla
½ teaspoon salt
2 tablespoons lemon juice
3 eggs, beaten
1 cup light cream

Preheat the oven to 450° F.

Roll the pie crust, line the pan, and prick the shell on the bottom and sides with a fork. Bake 10 minutes, remove from the oven, and lower the heat to 375° F.

Mix the sweet potatoes and sugar.

Add the butter, nutmeg, mace, vanilla, salt, and lemon juice; mix well.

Gradually add the eggs and cream; mix until smooth.

Pour the mixture into the partially baked pie shell.

Bake the pie at 375° F. for 35 to 40 minutes or until a knife inserted in the center comes out clean.

LEMON CHESS TARTS

(12 small tarts)

This originally was a cake or a tart of light pastry containing cheese and was often mentioned from around 1440 onward. Over the years, however, the cheese disappeared from the recipe, and lemon or orange and almonds were substituted. But the word "chess," a housewifely corruption of "cheese," has remained in the name to this day.

PASTRY CRUST MIX *for 12 tart*
   shells (page 133)
1¾ cups sugar
6 to 8 tablespoons lemon juice

rind of 2 lemons, grated
½ cup butter
6 eggs, well beaten

Prepare and bake 12 tart shells.

Mix the sugar, juice, and rind.

Melt the butter in the top of a double boiler. Add the sugar mixture and eggs.

Continue cooking over hot water until very thick, stirring constantly.

Cool, cover, and refrigerate.

When chilled, fill the tart shells.

138

PECAN PIE

(one 9-inch pie)

The pecan tree, native to the banks of the Illinois and Mississippi rivers, fascinated Thomas Jefferson. Many times he wrote to his friends requesting some nuts: "I shall set great value on the chance of having a grove of them." In time, he planted hundreds of pecan trees and was generous in giving nuts to his friends. On March 25, 1775, George Washington planted at Mount Vernon pecans that Jefferson had sent him. Three of the trees are still growing on the banks of the Potomac. According to tradition, some of the pecan trees at the St. George Tucker House in Williamsburg grew from pecans Jefferson gave Tucker.

PASTRY CRUST MIX *for 9-inch*
  pie shell (page 133)
4 eggs
¾ cup sugar
½ teaspoon salt

1½ cups light corn syrup
1 tablespoon butter, melted
1 teaspoon vanilla
1 cup pecan halves

Preheat oven to 400° F.

Prepare pie shell.

Beat the eggs lightly and add the sugar, salt, corn syrup, cooled butter, and vanilla; stir until mixed well.

Spread the pecan halves on the bottom crust and cover with the filling.

Place in the oven and immediately reduce the heat to 350° F.

Bake for 40 to 50 minutes or until the mixture is firm in the center.

Cool before serving.

BICENTENNIAL TART

(12–14 servings)

PASTRY CRUST MIX *for 10-inch pie shell (page 133)*

1 pound dried beans

VANILLA CREAM CUSTARD *(page 141)*

SPONGECAKE *(page 141)*

3 tablespoons sugar, divided

¼ cup water

4 tablespoons kirsch

2 pints fresh strawberries, washed and hulled

2 medium bananas, sliced and brushed with lemon juice

½ pint fresh blueberries, washed and hulled, or ½ can blueberry pie filling

1 cup apricot jam, forced through a sieve

1 tablespoon brandy

½ cup almonds, sliced and toasted

Preheat the oven to 375° F.

Grease a 10-inch tart pan 1½ inches deep and line it with the dough. Prick the bottom and sides with a fork. Place greased wax paper over the dough and fill with dried beans to prevent the dough from rising.

Bake at 375° F. for 35 minutes. Remove from the oven, empty the beans, remove the wax paper, prick the bottom, and return to the oven for about 5 minutes or until the shell is a golden brown.

Place on a rack and cool.

Line the bottom of the cooled tart shell with the Vanilla Cream Custard.

Make a sugar syrup by dissolving 2 tablespoons of sugar in ¼ cup of water. Bring to a boil, remove from the heat, and add the kirsch.

Place the Spongecake on top of the custard and slowly spoon the sugar syrup over the surface of the cake.

Beginning at the outside edge of the tart, put on 2 rows of strawberries, hulled ends down. Add a row of overlapping banana slices, and fill the center with blueberries.

In a small saucepan, bring the apricot jam and 1 tablespoon of sugar to a boil, stirring constantly. Remove from the heat and add the brandy.

Spoon the glaze over the fruit.

Paint the sides of the tart with the glaze and press on the almonds.

VANILLA CREAM CUSTARD

5 egg yolks
½ cup sugar
2 tablespoons cornstarch

2 cups milk
1 teaspoon vanilla

Beat the egg yolks and sugar rapidly to blend well.

In a saucepan, dissolve the cornstarch in ½ cup of milk. Add the rest of the milk and the vanilla and bring to a boil, stirring constantly.

Pour gradually into the egg mixture and blend well.

Return to the heat and boil, stirring constantly, 2 minutes.

Cool in the refrigerator until needed.

SPONGECAKE

3 eggs, separated
½ cup sugar
1 teaspoon vanilla
pinch of cream of tartar

⅔ cup cake flour, measured
    after sifting
4 tablespoons butter, melted
    and cooled slightly

Preheat the oven to 350° F.

Grease well and lightly flour the bottom and sides of a 9-inch round cake pan.

Beat the egg yolks for 1 minute, then gradually add the sugar and beat for 4 minutes. Add the vanilla.

Beat the egg whites until foamy, add the pinch of cream of tartar, and beat on high speed until they form very stiff peaks.

Lightly and delicately fold ¼ of the whites into the yolks mixture. Then fold in ⅓ of the flour, ¼ of the whites, ⅓ of the flour, ¼ of the whites, ⅓ of the flour, and the remaining ¼ of the whites.

Add the butter, folding just enough to mix well. Pour into the prepared pan.

Bake at 350° F. for 20 minutes or until done. Do not overbake. Cool in the pan 10 minutes, then turn out onto a rack.

Cakes and Frostings

Great-great-grandmother's cake recipes can sound appalling as well as amusing; the cakemaker of today is infinitely luckier than the cakemaker of ancestral days.

The number of eggs called for in the old recipes seems needlessly extravagant, until we recall that colonial hens, which had to scratch for their living, laid much smaller eggs than do their scientifically bred, fed, pampered, and confined successors of this century. Egg yolks and whites were then beaten with forks or hickory rods—think of the length of time it took to beat the eggs for big cakes! It was a lucky day for housewives when an egg beater was patented in 1870. Marion Harland, author of *Common Sense in the Household*, who bought her egg beater in 1871, could thereafter turn out a meringue in five minutes, she testified, and make "snow custard in less than half an hour with no tremulousness of nerve or tendon."

Sugar, imported from the West Indies in colonial times, was costly and came in large, cone-shaped loaves, which had to be broken down. Among the cakes then popular was the "black cake that will last a year" if properly stored—the forerunner of the Christmas cakes and puddings of today.

Tempting baked treats include Indian Corn ▶ Sticks and Muffins and golden Sally Lunn bread.

142

LAYER CAKE
(three 9-inch layers)

1½ cups butter   3 teaspoons baking powder
2 cups sugar   1 teaspoon salt
4 eggs   1 cup milk
3 cups sifted cake flour   1 teaspoon vanilla

Preheat the oven to 350° F.

Grease three 9-inch cake pans and dust them lightly with flour.

Cream the butter and sugar.

Add 1 egg at a time, beating well after each addition.

Sift the dry ingredients together and add alternately with the milk and vanilla.

Pour into the prepared pans and bake at 350° F. for 20 to 25 minutes.

Cool and frost with Caramel Frosting (page 151); Chocolate Frosting (page 152); Sea Foam Frosting (page 152); Seven-Minute Frosting (page 153); or Sherry Frosting (page 153).

LAYER CAKE
(two 9-inch layers)

1 cup butter   2½ teaspoons baking powder
1⅓ cups sugar   ¾ teaspoon salt
2 eggs   ¾ cup milk
2½ cups sifted cake flour   1 teaspoon vanilla

Follow the instructions for the 3-layer cake (*above*), but use two 9-inch pans.

◄ *Homemade ice cream served with Williamsburg Inn Pecan Bars is a popular choice for dessert on the shady terrace of the Williamsburg Inn on a summer afternoon. Shown here are: Orange Sherbet, Peppermint Stick Ice Cream, Rum Raisin Ice Cream, Chowning's Tavern Black Walnut Ice Cream, Vanilla Ice Cream, Lemon Ice, Raspberry Ice, and King's Arms Tavern Greengage Plum Ice Cream.*

WILLIAMSBURG LODGE
ORANGE WINE CAKE

½ cup butter
½ cup shortening
1½ cups sugar
4 eggs
1½ cups buttermilk
3½ cups sifted cake flour,
    divided
2 teaspoons baking soda

½ teaspoon salt
2 teaspoons orange extract
1 tablespoon orange rind,
    grated
1 cup raisins, finely chopped
1 cup pecans, finely chopped
SHERRY FROSTING (*page 153*)

Preheat the oven to 350° F.

Lightly grease and flour two 9-inch round or three 8-inch round cake pans.

Cream the butter, shortening, and sugar.

Gradually beat in the eggs and buttermilk alternately with the sifted dry ingredients. Add the orange extract and orange rind.

Scrape down the bowl occasionally and mix until smooth.

Dredge the chopped raisins in ¼ cup of flour. Add the raisins and pecans to the mixture.

Pour the batter into the prepared pans.

Bake at 350° F. for 30 minutes for 9-inch layers, 35 minutes for 8-inch layers, or until the cake tests done.

Remove from the oven and cool 5 minutes in the pans. Turn out on cooling racks and finish cooling.

Frost with Sherry Frosting.

BANANA CAKE

2 cups sifted all-purpose flour
1 teaspoon baking powder
1 teaspoon baking soda
¾ teaspoon salt
1⅓ cups sugar
½ cup shortening

½ cup milk
1 cup ripe bananas, mashed
½ cup buttermilk
2 eggs
½ cup nuts, chopped

Preheat the oven to 350° F.

Grease and flour a 10 x 5 x 3-inch pan.

Sift the dry ingredients into a mixing bowl and add the shortening, milk, bananas, and buttermilk. Beat 2 minutes on low to medium speed of an electric mixer, scraping the bowl as needed.

Add the eggs and beat 1 minute more.

Stir in the nuts.

Pour into the prepared cake pan and bake for 45 to 50 minutes at 350° F. or until the cake tests done when pressed lightly in the center.

Cool in the pan 10 minutes before turning out onto a rack.

BOURBON PECAN CAKE

2 teaspoons nutmeg, freshly
   grated
½ cup bourbon
1½ cups sifted all-purpose
   flour, divided
2 cups pecans, finely chopped
1 cup seedless raisins, finely
   chopped

⅓ cup butter
1 cup plus 2 tablespoons sugar
3 eggs, separated
1½ teaspoons baking powder
dash of salt
pecan halves
maraschino cherries

Preheat the oven to 325° F.

Line the bottom of a 10-inch tube cake pan with brown paper and grease it.

Soak the nutmeg in the bourbon.

Mix ½ cup of flour with the nuts and raisins, coating thoroughly. Reserve.

Cream the butter and sugar until light and fluffy.

Add the egg yolks, one at a time, beating well after each addition.

Beat in the remaining flour and the baking powder and salt.

Beat in the bourbon-nutmeg mixture and continue beating until the batter is well mixed.

Add the floured nuts and raisins and mix well so that they are evenly distributed in the batter.

Beat the egg whites until very stiff. Fold in.

Spoon the batter into the prepared pan. Press down firmly to squeeze out any air pockets and allow to stand 10 minutes.

Decorate the top with the pecan halves and drained maraschino cherries.

Bake at 325° F. for 1 to 1¼ hours or until the cake tests done.

Cool in the pan, right side up, 1 to 2 hours before turning out. Continue cooling.

Note: This cake improves with age. Wrap it in a napkin that has been soaked in bourbon and store in a covered container for several days.

DEVIL'S FOOD CAKE

1½ cups milk, divided
4 ounces unsweetened
   chocolate
1½ cups sugar, divided
½ cup butter

1 teaspoon vanilla
2 eggs
¾ teaspoon salt
2 cups sifted all-purpose flour
1 teaspoon baking soda

Preheat the oven to 350° F.

Line the bottoms of two 9-inch cake pans with waxed or brown paper. Grease and flour the pans.

Heat 1 cup of milk with the chocolate and ½ cup of sugar in the top of a double boiler or heavy saucepan, stirring constantly until smooth; cool.

Cream the butter and remaining sugar in the large bowl of an electric mixer.

Add the vanilla and eggs and beat well.

Beat in the cooled chocolate mixture.

Sift the salt with the flour and add alternately with the remaining milk, then beat 2 minutes at medium speed before adding the baking soda dissolved in 3 tablespoons of boiling water.

Beat 1 minute longer.

Pour into the prepared pans.

Bake at 350° F. for 25 to 30 minutes or until the cake tests done.

Cool in the pans 10 minutes; remove from the pans and finish cooling on racks.

Frost with Caramel Frosting (page 151), Chocolate Frosting (page 152), or Seven-Minute Frosting (page 153).

BLACK FOREST CAKE
(12–14 servings)

Fudge Cake *(page 148)*
1 can (17 ounces) pitted dark
   sweet cherries
2 tablespoons cornstarch
3 cups whipping cream
½ cup confectioner's sugar

⅓ cup kirsch, divided
2 cups Chocolate Frosting
   (page 152)
semisweet bar chocolate,
   shaved or grated
maraschino cherries, stemmed

Preheat the oven to 325° F.

Bake the cake in three 9-inch layers at 325° F. for 30 to 35 minutes, or until the cake tests done. Cool 10 minutes in the pans, then turn out on racks to finish cooling.

Drain the liquid from the cherries into a small saucepan; reserve the cherries.

Bring the liquid to a boil. Mix the cornstarch with ¼ cup of water and stir it into the juice. Cook until clear.

Add the cherries; cool.

Whip the cream until soft peaks form. Sprinkle the sugar over the cream and continue beating until firm peaks form on the beater when it is lifted from the bowl.

Pour in ¼ cup of kirsch a little at a time, beating only until it is taken up by the cream.

Place one layer of the cake on a large cake plate.

Use a plain ½-inch tube or the plain nozzle of a cookie press to form 3 rings of Chocolate Butter Cream Frosting on the bottom layer, leaving about 1½ inches between the rings. Chill.

Fill in between the rings with the cherries.

Place the second layer gently on top of the cherries.

Prick the top all over with a fork, sprinkle it lightly with kirsch, and spread it with 1 inch of whipped cream.

Put the top layer on gently. Spread the sides and top with the remaining whipped cream.

Garnish the top with chocolate curls, a whipped cream rosette or dollop of whipped cream, and the maraschino cherries, rinsed and drained.

Refrigerate until serving time.

FUDGE CAKE

1 cup butter	*1½ teaspoons baking soda*
2 cups sugar	*⅔ cup buttermilk*
4 eggs	*1 teaspoon vanilla*
2 cups sifted all-purpose flour	*3 ounces unsweetened*
¼ teaspoon salt	*chocolate, grated*

Preheat the oven to 325° F.

Grease and flour a 9 x 13 x 1½-inch pan.

Cream the butter and sugar.

Add the eggs one at a time and beat well after each addition.

After the last egg has been added, beat for 1 minute or until the mixture is light and fluffy.

Sift the flour with the salt.

148

Mix the baking soda with the buttermilk and add alternately with the flour to the creamed mixture.

Add the vanilla.

Melt the chocolate in ⅔ cup of boiling water; stir until smooth.

Blend the chocolate into the cake mixture.

Pour into the prepared pan and bake for 1 hour at 325° F. or until the cake tests done.

Cool in the pan.

Frost while slightly warm with Chocolate Frosting (page 152).

ORANGE BLOSSOMS
(6 dozen)

3 eggs	*½ teaspoon salt*
1½ cups sugar	*4 tablespoons butter, melted*
1 teaspoon vanilla	*and cooled slightly*
1½ cups sifted all-purpose flour	ORANGE SYRUP *(below)*
2 teaspoons baking powder	

Preheat the oven to 400° F.

Grease muffin tins that are 1½ inches in diameter.

Beat the eggs until very light. Add the sugar gradually, beating until the mixture is well blended.

Add ½ cup of cold water and the vanilla. Fold in the sifted dry ingredients.

Fold in the melted butter.

Fill the muffin tins ¾ full. Bake at 400° F. for 12 minutes.

Immediately remove the Orange Blossoms from the muffin tins and dip them in the Orange Syrup. Drain on a rack.

ORANGE SYRUP

2½ cups granulated sugar	*6 tablespoons lemon juice*
1 cup orange juice	

Combine the ingredients and bring to a boil.

Cool and refrigerate 24 hours before using.

SPICY CARROT CAKE

1½ cups vegetable oil
2½ cups sugar
4 eggs, separated
2½ cups sifted all-purpose flour
1½ teaspoons baking powder
½ teaspoon baking soda
¼ teaspoon salt

½ teaspoon nutmeg
1 teaspoon cinnamon
1 teaspoon ground cloves
1½ cups raw carrots, grated
1 cup pecans, chopped
GLAZE *(below)*

Preheat the oven to 350° F.

Grease and flour a 10-inch tube cake pan.

Mix the oil and sugar together. Beat in the egg yolks one at a time. Continue to beat and add 5 tablespoons of hot water.

Sift together the flour, baking powder, baking soda, salt, and spices. Add to the egg mixture.

Stir in the carrots and pecans.

Beat the egg whites until they form stiff peaks; fold in.

Pour the batter into the prepared pan and bake at 350° F. for 60 to 70 minutes or until the cake tests done.

Cool in the pan right side up for 15 minutes, then turn out to finish cooling on a cake rack.

Drizzle the Glaze in a circle on top of the cake.

GLAZE

¾ cup sifted confectioner's sugar

3 tablespoons lemon juice

Mix the above ingredients together to make a glaze.

POUND CAKE

1 cup butter
1 cup sugar
6 eggs
2 cups sifted all-purpose flour

½ teaspoon baking powder
1 teaspoon orange flavoring
1 teaspoon lemon flavoring

Have all of the ingredients at room temperature.

Preheat the oven to 325° F.

Grease and dust with flour a 9¼ x 5¼ x 2¾-inch loaf pan or a 9-inch tube pan.

Cream the butter and gradually add the sugar. Add the eggs one at a time, beating well after each addition.

Sift the flour and baking powder together and gradually stir into the egg mixture.

Add the orange and lemon flavorings.

Spoon into the prepared pan.

Bake at 325° F. for 70 minutes if a loaf pan is used or 60 minutes for a tube pan.

Cool in the pan 10 minutes, then finish cooling on a rack.

WILLIAMSBURG INN
DATE NUT POUND CAKE

⅓ cup chopped pecans or
   walnuts

⅓ cup chopped dates

Follow the recipe for Pound Cake (page 150), except reserve 2 tablespoons of the flour to dredge the dates.

After adding the dry ingredients to the egg mixture, stir in the pecans or walnuts and dates.

CARAMEL FROSTING
(for 2-layer cake)

¼ cup butter
¾ cup light brown sugar,
   packed
¼ cup evaporated milk

2½ to 3 cups sifted
   confectioner's sugar
1 teaspoon vanilla
dash of salt

Melt the butter in a saucepan over medium heat and add the brown sugar and milk. Heat until the sugar dissolves.

Cool slightly, then beat in the confectioner's sugar, vanilla, and salt.

Double the recipe to frost a 3-layer cake.

Use with Layer Cake (page 143), or Devil's Food Cake (page 146).

CHOCOLATE FROSTING

(for 2-layer cake)

4 ounces unsweetened
  chocolate
½ cup butter
3 cups sifted confectioner's
  sugar

dash of salt
1 teaspoon vanilla
½ to ⅔ cup evaporated milk

Melt the chocolate and butter over hot water.

Sift the sugar and salt together and add the vanilla and chocolate mixture.

Add enough milk to make spreading consistency.

Increase the ingredients by ½ to frost a 3-layer cake.

Use with Layer Cake (page 143), Devil's Food Cake (page 146), or Fudge Cake (page 148).

SEA FOAM FROSTING

(for 2-layer cake)

2 egg whites
¼ teaspoon cream of tartar
dash of salt

1½ cups light brown sugar,
  packed
1 teaspoon vanilla

Beat the egg whites at moderate speed until foamy. Add the cream of tartar and salt and beat at high speed until stiff peaks form.

Combine the brown sugar with ½ cup of water and stir over low heat until the sugar is dissolved.

Bring the mixture to a boil, stirring and cooking until the mixture spins a thread (236° F. on a candy thermometer).

Pour the sugar mixture over the beaten egg whites, beating constantly. Do not scrape the pan but allow the cooked mixture to run out.

Add the vanilla and continue beating until of spreading consistency.

Double the recipe to frost a 3-layer cake.

Use with Layer Cake (page 143).

SEVEN-MINUTE FROSTING
(for 2-layer cake)

2 egg whites
1 tablespoon light corn syrup
  or ¼ teaspoon cream of tartar

1½ cups sugar
1 teaspoon vanilla

Combine all of the ingredients except the vanilla in ⅓ cup of water in the top of a double boiler.

Beat until well blended, about 1 minute on high speed of an electric beater.

Place over rapidly boiling water and beat constantly for 5 to 8 minutes or until the mixture forms soft peaks.

Remove from the water and add the vanilla. Turn the frosting into a bowl and continue to beat for 2 minutes.

Double the recipe to frost a 3-layer cake.

Use with Layer Cake (page 143) or Devil's Food Cake (page 146).

SHERRY FROSTING
(for 2-layer cake)

¼ cup butter
2½ to 3 cups sifted
  confectioner's sugar
¼ cup orange juice

½ teaspoon orange flavoring
dash of salt
½ teaspoon orange rind, grated
dry sherry

Cream the butter and add the remaining ingredients except the sherry.

Add enough sherry, approximately 1 tablespoon, to make the frosting of spreading consistency. If the frosting is too thin, add more sugar or refrigerate it.

Double the recipe to frost a 3-layer cake.

Use with Layer Cake (page 143), or Williamsburg Lodge Orange Wine Cake (page 144).

Cookies

BOURBON BALLS

(36–42 balls)

2 cups vanilla wafer crumbs
2 tablespoons cocoa
1½ cups confectioner's sugar,
   divided

1 cup pecans, very finely
   chopped
2 tablespoons white corn syrup
¼ cup bourbon

Mix well the vanilla wafer crumbs, cocoa, 1 cup of confectioner's sugar, and pecans.

Add the corn syrup and bourbon; mix well.

Shape into 1-inch balls and roll in the remaining confectioner's sugar.

Put in a tightly covered tin box or other metal container for at least 12 hours before serving.

Note: These cookies keep well for 4 or 5 weeks.

RUM BALLS

(36–42 balls)

Follow the recipe for Bourbon Balls *(above)*.
Substitute ¼ cup of rum for the bourbon.

BRANDY BALLS

(36–42 balls)

Follow the recipe for Bourbon Balls *(above)*.
Substitute ¼ cup of brandy for the bourbon.

155

CINNAMON SQUARES

(48 squares)

½ cup butter
½ cup margarine
1 cup sugar
1 egg, separated

2 cups sifted all-purpose flour
1½ tablespoons cinnamon
1 teaspoon salt
1½ cups nuts, chopped

Preheat the oven to 325° F.
Grease and flour a 15½ x 10½ x 1-inch pan.
Cream the butter, margarine, and sugar. Add the egg yolk and sifted dry ingredients.
Press the batter into the prepared pan.
Beat the egg white until foamy and spread it sparingly over the batter.
Press on the nuts.
Bake at 325° F. for 30 minutes.
Cut into squares.

CHOWNING'S TAVERN BROWNIES

(20 brownies)

1 cup butter
8 ounces unsweetened
  chocolate
7 eggs
3 cups sugar

½ teaspoon vanilla
2 cups sifted all-purpose
  flour
1 tablespoon baking powder
2 cups pecans, chopped

Preheat the oven to 350° F.
Grease a 10½ x 15½ x 1-inch pan.
Melt the butter and chocolate in a double boiler over hot water.
Beat the eggs, sugar, and vanilla until frothy.
Add the melted butter and chocolate.
Add the sifted dry ingredients. Stir in the pecans.
Pour into the prepared pan and bake at 350° F. for 30 minutes.
Cool and cut into 3 x 3-inch squares.

HOLIDAY COOKIES

(36 cookies)

½ cup butter, softened
1 cup sugar
1 egg, beaten
1 teaspoon vanilla
1 tablespoon whipping cream

2 cups sifted all-purpose flour
1½ teaspoons baking powder
½ teaspoon salt
colored sugar

Preheat the oven to 375° F. 10 minutes before the cookies are ready to go in.

Grease a cookie sheet.

Cream the butter and sugar. Add the egg, vanilla, cream, and sifted dry ingredients.

Wrap the dough in plastic wrap and chill in the refrigerator several hours.

Roll out, cut, and sprinkle with the colored sugar.

Place at least 3 inches apart on the prepared cookie sheet (they spread quite a bit).

Bake at 375° F. for 15 minutes.

Note: If not served immediately, store in a covered container to retain crispness.

ORANGE NUT BARS

(21–28 bars)

3 eggs
1 can (6 ounces) frozen orange
    juice concentrate
1 cup sugar
2 cups graham cracker crumbs
1 teaspoon baking powder

¼ teaspoon salt
1 cup chopped nuts
1 package (8 ounces) pitted
    dates, chopped
1 teaspoon vanilla
ORANGE ICING *(page 158)*

Preheat the oven to 350° F.

Grease and lightly flour a 9-inch-square pan.

Beat the eggs until light and fluffy. Beat in the orange juice concentrate. Stir in the remaining ingredients and mix well.

Spoon the mixture into the prepared pan.

Bake at 350° F. for 50 minutes.

Remove from the oven and cool in the pan on a rack.

Frost with Orange Icing and cut into bars.

ORANGE ICING

1¼ cups confectioner's sugar   2½ tablespoons orange juce

Beat until smooth and ready to spread.

WILLIAMSBURG INN
PECAN BARS

(54 bars)

¾ cup butter
¾ cup sugar
2 eggs
rind of 1 lemon, grated

3 cups sifted all-purpose flour
½ teaspoon baking powder
PECAN TOPPING *(page 159)*

Preheat the oven to 375° F. 10 minutes before the dough is ready to go in.

Grease and flour two 9 x 9 x 2-inch baking pans.

Cream the butter and sugar; add the eggs and lemon rind and beat well.

Sift the flour and baking powder together; add to the creamed mixture and beat well.

Chill the dough until it is firm enough to handle.

Press the dough onto the bottom of the prepared pans. The dough will be approximately ⅛-inch thick. Prick all over with a fork.

Bake 12 to 15 minutes at 375° F. or until the dough looks half done.

Remove from the oven and follow the instructions under Pecan Topping (page 159).

In the soft glow of candlelight, the dining room of the George Wythe House is set once again with tempting eighteenth-century desserts—three Pound Cakes baked in Turk's-head molds, Ambrosia (center), Pecan Pie, Apple Dumplings, and Wine Jelly Molds, with marzipan filling the top glass. Sweetmeats and fruit are arranged on the creamware épergne.

▶

PECAN TOPPING

(54 bars)

1 cup butter
1 cup light brown sugar,
  packed

1 cup honey
¼ cup whipping cream
3 cups pecans, chopped

Preheat the oven to 350° F.

Put the butter, sugar, and honey in a deep, heavy saucepan; boil, stirring, 5 minutes. Remove from the heat.

Cool slightly and add the cream and chopped pecans; mix well.

Spread the topping evenly over the surface of the partially baked sugar dough (page 158) with a buttered wooden spoon or flexible spatula.

Bake for 30 to 35 minutes at 350° F.

Cool and cut into 1 x 2-inch bars.

◀ *The Raleigh Tavern bar, where many a colonial gentleman quenched his thirst, is the background for a variety of typical Williamsburg beverages. Left to right: Chowning's Tavern Wine Cooler, Eggnog, Champagne Punch, Wine Punch, Fish House Punch, and Sherry.*

Beverages

Alcoholic beverages were a household staple in colonial Virginia. There were no aspirins, no tranquilizers, and no anesthetics, so brandy or rum often was used in their stead. Too, a good drink was regarded as a preventive against flux and fever, which is why many an early rising planter fortified himself with a starter before making the rounds of his plantation.

Rare was the Virginia gentleman, however, who failed to conduct himself with "great Decency and good Order," drinks or no drinks. Gentlemen had to set an example. Else how could they hope to keep the field hands and servants sober? "The parson and I returned to our quarters in good time and good order," wrote William Byrd on March 2, 1728, "but my man Tom broke the rules of hospitality by getting extremely drunk in a civil house." It was a problem.

Thomas Jefferson was an acknowledged connoisseur of foreign wines. He supported a proposed reduction of duties on wine to avoid the use of whiskey as a substitute. Wine he declared to be a necessity of life and said no nation is drunk where wine is cheap.

Claret was Washington's favorite wine. When the Marquis de Chastellux presented him with a cask, Washington replied, "You can relieve me by promising to partake very often of that hilarity which a Glass of good Claret seldom fails to produce."

CHOWNING'S TAVERN
WINE COOLER

(1 serving)

¾ *glass lemonade*　　　　　　*sprig of mint*
¼ *glass dry red wine*　　　　　*maraschino cherry*

This makes a colorful as well as refreshing drink if the liquids are not mixed together. Pour the lemonade over crushed ice, then add the red wine.

Garnish with a sprig of mint and a cherry.

Good for hot days.

PUNCH

Although much was said in praise of wine, more was said of punch. This was the Tidewater's standby drink. "Punch" is the English rendering of the Hindustani *pauch*, meaning five, for the five ingredients—spirits, water, sliced lemons or limes, sugar, and spice.

Ned Ward, an eighteenth-century English tavern-keeper and satirist, intoxicated by the merits of this concoction, penned the following couplet in its praise:

> Immortal Drink, whose compound is of Five,
> More praise dost thou deserve than man can give.

The recipe for the immortal drink came to England from the Far East, together with tea, root ginger, and spice, fine East Indian muslins and cashmere shawls, and other new delights, either by way of the fourteenth-century caravan route or by sea around the Cape of Good Hope.

In the Tidewater, rum from the West Indies and brandy were the chief ingredients of punch. In December 1710 William Byrd II described the afternoon's activity: "My wife and I made some punch of [lemons] white sack, and Madeira brandy, and I put it into bottles."

A bowl of punch was the planter's most companionable drink. Many a political strategy was hatched, many a long evening of pleasure was spent with a small punch bowl at each right elbow. The punch made by one of Williamsburg's tavern-keepers, Henry Wetherburn, figures in a story that is still remembered today. In May 1736, after planter William Randolph agreed to sell some of his farm land to Thomas Jefferson's father, he insisted on Henry Wetherburn's "biggest bowl of Arrack punch" to seal the bargain.

WINE PUNCH

(12 servings)

1 bottle red wine
1 cup orange juice
1 cup pineapple juice

2 lemons, sliced
3 oranges, sliced

Combine all of the ingredients and pour over a block of ice.

CHAMPAGNE PUNCH

(15 servings)

1 bottle champagne, chilled
½ cup brandy
½ cup Cointreau

½ bottle sparkling water,
*   chilled*

Combine all of the ingredients and serve in punch cups.

FISH HOUSE PUNCH

(10–15 servings)

1 cup light brown sugar,
*   packed*
9 lemons
2 cups pineapple juice

1 fifth dark rum
½ fifth cognac
4 tablespoons peach brandy

Mix the sugar and 4 cups of water in a pan and boil 5 minutes.

Squeeze the juice from the lemons and pour it into the hot syrup. Add the lemon rinds.

Cool the syrup and refrigerate overnight.

Just before serving, remove the lemon rinds. Add the pineapple juice and liquors.

Pack a large punch bowl with crushed ice. Pour the punch over the ice and serve.

HOT SPICED PUNCH

(8 servings)

1 quart apple cider
3 cinnamon sticks
4 tablespoons lemon juice

1 teaspoon nutmeg
1 teaspoon whole cloves

Simmer the cider, cinnamon sticks, and lemon juice for 15 minutes.

Tie the nutmeg and cloves in a small cheesecloth bag and put it into the simmering cider long enough to give it the desired taste.

WASSAIL

(20 servings)

Wassailing is an ancient English custom, part of the feasts and revelry of New Year's Eve and New Year's Day, which have been revived in Colonial Williamsburg. The master of the English household drank the health of those present with a bowl of spiced ale, and each in turn after him passed the bowl along and repeated the Saxon phrase *Wass hael*, "be whole," or "be well."

1 cup sugar	*6 cups dry red wine*
4 cinnamon sticks	*½ cup lemon juice*
3 lemon slices	*1 cup dry sherry*
2 cups pineapple juice	*2 lemons, sliced*
2 cups orange juice	

Boil the sugar, cinnamon sticks, and 3 lemon slices in ½ cup of water for 5 minutes and strain. Discard the cinnamon sticks and lemon slices.

Heat but do not boil the remaining ingredients.

Combine with the syrup, garnish with the lemon slices, and serve hot.

EGGNOG

(*12 cups*)

The drink called eggnog in America may be an adaptation of milk punch, an old English drink made with milk, eggs, brandy, sugar, and lemon juice. In February 1796, Isaac Weld wrote that he and several other travelers who had stopped in Philadelphia at the same house all breakfasted together: "The American travellers, before they pursued their journey, took a hearty draught each, according to custom, of egg-nog, a mixture composed of new milk, eggs, rum, and sugar, beat up together."

6 eggs, separated	*½ cup bourbon*
½ cup sugar	*½ cup brandy*
2 cups whipping cream	*½ cup light rum*
1 cup milk	*nutmeg*

Beat the egg yolks with the sugar until thick.
Slowly add the cream, milk, and spirits.
Chill.

Whip the egg whites until soft peaks form and add to the mixture.

Chill and let ripen a few hours.

Sprinkle with nutmeg before serving.

Index

Entries in *italics* refer to illustrations on facing page unless otherwise noted

Index

Index

173